I0199915

Scattering Ashes

Scattering Ashes

A Sister's Journey With Her Gay Brother

JOYCE SMITH HELYER

RESOURCE *Publications* • Eugene, Oregon

SCATTERING ASHES
A Sister's Journey With Her Gay Brother

Copyright © 2016 Joyce Smith Helyer. All rights reserved. Except for brief quotations in critical publications or reviews, no part of this book may be reproduced in any manner without prior written permission from the publisher. Write: Permissions, Wipf and Stock Publishers, 199 W. 8th Ave., Suite 3, Eugene, OR 97401.

Resource Publications
An Imprint of Wipf and Stock Publishers
199 W. 8th Ave., Suite 3
Eugene, OR 97401

www.wipfandstock.com

PAPERBACK ISBN: 978-1-4982-8976-4
HARDCOVER ISBN: 978-1-4982-8978-8
EBOOK ISBN: 978-1-4982-8977-1

Manufactured in the U.S.A.   05/25/16

People Need the Lord. Words and Music by Greg Nelson and Phill McHugh. Copyright 1983 Shepherd's Fold Music (BMI) River Oaks Music Company (BMI) (adm. at CapitolCMGPublishing.com). All rights reserved. Used by permission.

Case Studies. *Loving Lesbian Neighbors* and *Should We Attend this Party?* by Denis Haack of Ransom Fellowship, 5245 132nd Court, Savage, MN 55378, info@ransomfellowship.org. Used by permission.

Scripture quotations taken from the *Holy Bible, New International Version.* Copyright 1973, 1978, 1984 by International Bible Society. Used by permission of Zondervan Publishing House.

To my husband Larry
whose acts of love, grace, and mercy
sustained me throughout the journey.

The center to which Christians turn to find our bearings, whether about race or sexuality, is the cross of Jesus Christ—the story of God's righteous and merciful love.

—MARK LABBERTON,
President, Fuller Theological Seminary

Contents

Acknowledgments | ix
Introduction | xi

1 Keeping Secrets | 1
2 The Early Years | 10
3 The Turning Point | 23
4 Cries for Help | 40
5 Death Came Knocking | 51
6 Mom, Is Uncle Ron Gay? | 61
7 The Elephant in the Room | 67
8 Extending Grace and Mercy | 75

CASE STUDIES

CASE STUDY #1
Loving Lesbian Neighbors | 105
   by Denis Haack

CASE STUDY #2
Our Son Is Gay | 108

CASE STUDY #3
Should We Attend This Party? | 114
   by Denis Haack

CASE STUDY #4
Sam and Roger | 118

For Further Study | 121

ACKNOWLEDGMENTS

I HAVE NOT TRAVELED this journey alone. Many came alongside during the years of internal debate about writing Ron's story and my journey with him. Following a chapel service in 2005 when I publicly told my story for the first time, colleagues Dr. Faye Chechowich Schroeder and Dr. Stephen Bedi from Taylor University planted the seed when they approached me and encouraged me to write a book about my journey with Ron so others with gay loved ones might find help and insight. That conversation led me to consider undertaking this project, but it was still some years before I started writing.

Without the support of my husband Larry, my children Alicia Brummeler (thank you for your expert assistance with editing selected chapters), son Nate, and son-in-law Brad, I would not have had the courage to attempt this task. An enthusiastic email from Brad at just the right moment encouraged me to move forward and helped me to persevere. Many thanks to Linda Lambert for patiently wading through my first rough draft, and providing me with helpful and important suggestions. Other friends who read and commented on sections of the book included friends Denis Hensley (your professionalism and insights helped immensely), Katie Lehman, Mary Ellen Rothrock, Susan Hodge, Margaret Ashchoff, the Writers Bloc at Taylor University, Patryce Loftin, Dr. Julie Coburn, and Rachael Phillips (as a published author, your experience and counsel were much appreciated). Friend Carolyn

Guebert faithfully listened to my three chapel presentations and gave me the gift of her presence plus many encouraging words.

Thank you Ed Cyzewski, Christian author and blogger, for providing helpful edits and asking insightful questions as you walked me through how to improve and prepare my manuscript for publication. Dr. Heidi Lakanen, friend and walking partner, listened to my victories and sorrows throughout the writing process as we walked the Loop at Taylor. My sisters, Dorothy Stroup and Karon Forkus, were helpful resources as I clarified some events from our past. Dr. Gene Habecker and his wife Marylou believed in me and encouraged me to tell my story so that God could use it in the lives of others. On one of our trips to Israel with Taylor alumni and friends, Linda Jones was with us. On our last night in Israel she was asked to pray for me and my book project that God would use my story to help strengthen fellow believers with gay loved ones. Linda, I will never forget your prayer.

Many thanks to friends Tracy Hoskins, Sherri Harter, Cindy Huang, and Jenny Collins who would ask me "How's it going?" while offering words of encouragement to stay focused and complete the task. Appreciation must also be given to the women in my Food for Thought Bible Study. Your faithful prayers and expressions of support have made all the difference.

Thanks to all of you who unselfishly gave me the gift of time, lifted my spirits, and helped me to keep pressing forward. Last of all, I want to express thanks to my publisher Wipf & Stock for taking on this sensitive topic and especially my editor Matt Wimer for his patient and quick response to all my questions.

INTRODUCTION

WRITING *SCATTERING ASHES* HAS been a painful experience. Yet, it has been cathartic and healing at the same time, in spite of reliving difficult memories that were emotionally and physically exhausting. Life can be like that.

This is the story of my personal journey with Ron, my youngest and only male sibling. From the moment my parents brought Ron home from the hospital, I was elated to finally have a brother. The journey became a little more difficult to navigate the day Ron told me he was gay.

When I began writing, my goal was to tell Ron's story and my experiences with him so that Christian families who have gay loved ones might find hope, understanding, and comfort. After the initial shock of discovering their loved one is gay, often Christian families process this information by asking themselves painful questions. Some wonder how they can maintain a meaningful relationship with their loved one while remaining true to their faith commitment. "What does all of this mean?" I found myself struggling with similar questions. Parents and siblings sometimes ask themselves, "Did we do something wrong? What or who caused this? How could this happen in our Christian home?" It can be an emotional time. Feelings of guilt, anger, shame, embarrassment, and questioning how God could have allowed this to happen fill their minds. Some families wonder what their faith community will say when they hear the news.

These questions and concerns were part of my experience. Through years of Ron's late night phone calls and his despair, I found God's faithfulness and love sustaining me. Though our beliefs collided at times, I felt God wanted me to make myself available to Ron whenever he needed, in spite of the miles that separated us physically.

Initially filled with fear and sorrow, my journey soon changed to one of ministry. I came alongside my brother with a desire to support him emotionally and share God's redemptive love for him and others I came in contact with from the gay community. During those early years, homosexuality was a topic that was rarely discussed in my circles. My learning curve was steep and intense. That learning continues to this day.

While I never endorsed Ron's gay lifestyle, he knew I loved him. Understanding the depth of God's great love for Ron came to me over time. My head understood but my heart hurt. As I sought information and advice on how best to relate to Ron, I saw the life of Jesus as my pattern. I wanted to explore how Jesus related to hurting men and women he encountered during his earthly ministry. Some of these discoveries I share in chapter eight.

I felt compelled to write about Ron because I loved this compassionate and kind man who experienced a life that included joy, along with much heartache, and sickness. The unanticipated discovery of Ron's HIV status became his constant companion and formidable burden for over 11 years. My prayer is that others on similar journeys will find hope, understanding, and encouragement through my struggles and discoveries.

While writing *Scattering Ashes,* I came to the realization that Ron's story is not just about him but it's also about me and my spiritual journey through a difficult time. God used my experiences with Ron to help me see with new eyes a group of men and women who had been marginalized for so long that I rarely thought about them except when something appeared in the news. I had a lot to learn during those years. I added to my vocabulary new terms like *sexual orientation* and *gay lifestyle.* One constant remained throughout my journey—my love for Ron never wavered and my love for God grew.

After sharing my journey in a chapel service at Taylor University, the stimulus to write Ron's story became even stronger. I was challenged by conversations with students and staff who had loved ones who were gay and felt my comments had helped them. These conversations provided the impetus I needed to write my brother's story with the hope it could be a source of encouragement for those experiencing similar journeys with their loved ones.

I do not have answers for every question raised by those within the Christian community, but I'm not alone either. In order to help Christians deal with twenty-first century situations we may experience, I have included four case studies at the end of the book for those who would like to engage with others in further discussion in a small group setting, Sunday school class, or for their own individual reflection. Names and identifying details in the book and in the case studies have been changed to protect the privacy of individuals. A list of resources for further study is also included.

When I launched my journey of discovery I had no idea it would include this book and the opportunity to meet courageous men and women who were also walking alongside a gay family member. In spite of the emotional pain, I am grateful for what I discovered about myself, about Ron's struggles as a gay man, and about God's abundant grace and mercy. While standing on a mountaintop with my family scattering ashes, my journey with Ron did not end. Instead, my road toward increased understanding and helping others on their journey was just beginning.

1

Keeping Secrets

I will never forget that Christmas Eve—every vivid detail is etched in my memory. My parents' home was filled with the wonderful aroma of Christmas baking and the sounds of children's excited laughter.

My brother Ron had flown in from Oregon and our immediate family all gathered at our childhood home in California to celebrate Christmas. After stuffing ourselves with one of our favorite dinners and my mother's fruitcake, we watched all the grandkids act out the Christmas story. By that time we were tired and my two sisters were eager to get their little ones home and settled in bed. Since Ron and my family were the only ones staying overnight, we decided to stay up and chat after everyone else had gone to bed. The two of us sat comfortably together in our parents' living room. Ron chose the family easy chair while I lounged on the couch with my feet tucked under me. Speckled shadows cast by the colorful sparkling lights from the Christmas tree surrounded us. It was past midnight and the atmosphere felt warm and cozy.

Ron looked at me and said, "Joyce, I have something to tell you." As I waited expectantly for what he was going to say next, he paused, but then shifted the conversation. He tried again, but the same thing happened. I felt like he was trying to land an airplane in trouble and kept circling the airport looking for the best approach. His attempted landings kept falling short of the runway. A vague sense of uneasiness began to fill my mind.

Smiling at me, he repeated. "I have something to tell you." But he still couldn't bring himself to say it. Little did I realize that my nice "typical" Christian experience would be undergoing a significant change that night. Suddenly, suspicious thoughts from the distant past began to race wildly through my head. Fear I could barely articulate almost overwhelmed me.

Backing off again, Ron began to tell me about his current activities while I'm thinking, *What in the world is he trying to tell me that he can't bring himself to say?* All of a sudden I knew. My mind was running in a thousand different directions. It's strange what pops into your head when you feel a sense of growing fear. I thought back to the time when Ron went to prom and my mother described to me the long telephone conversations he had with his date. Surely that meant something, I thought. I felt like I was in a fog, grasping for bits of memory that would prove what I was beginning to sense could not be true—he was just confused.

As Ron continued talking, I felt my body growing tense. My heart was pounding. Finally, I looked at my handsome, 26 year-old brother and knew the words he was having so much difficulty saying. "Ron, are you trying to tell me you're gay?" His quiet response echoed across the living room. "I thought you had it figured out." He acted relieved. While I was trying to process what he had just confirmed, he proceeded to describe for me his former relationships, which included ministers he had been involved with sexually. Ron told me their interpretation of Scripture did not condemn homosexual activity. All the while I'm thinking, *I can't believe I'm hearing this.* I was afraid for him, for what my parents would think, what others would think, and especially concerned about his relationship with God.

How could this be happening? We'd grown up in a Christian family. Ron had trusted Christ as his Savior as a child and was baptized. Questions whirled in my mind. I felt sad and anxious. I silently called out to God for wisdom and the right words to say. If

I just said the right words, I thought I could help Ron see his need to change.

I chose my words carefully and told my brother I loved him, but homosexuality was wrong and not what God intended for him. After a long discussion between us, we agreed to disagree. Ron asked me not to tell our parents or my sisters unless they asked. This would be a major secret to keep. That wouldn't be a problem. I didn't want to tell anyone except my husband. I wasn't about to share this information with others. In the back of my mind was the image of the 1970s pop singer and Christian activist Anita Bryant and the attacks and confrontations she experienced from the gay community over her public statements opposing homosexuality.

It's hard keeping secrets. In fact, it's difficult living your whole life as one big secret. When Ron asked me to keep his secret I readily agreed to this because I thought it would be totally devastating if my family and friends ever discovered what he told me. I realize now I was wrong.

I climbed into bed that memorable Christmas Eve, but sleep did not come easily. My mind was racing, and I tossed and turned, all the time praying and asking God to change Ron. Even with Ron's admission that he was gay, I knew I loved him and would never separate myself from him. That question never entered my mind. However, I was struggling with what our relationship would look like if he never changed. This experience was totally new for me. I needed time to process all that was happening. I continued to go over in my mind how he told me he felt "different" as a child, and that he had already been involved sexually with men. This was troubling news to hear. What did Ron's disclosure mean for the future? My initial struggle revolved around how I could help Ron change. That became my focus. I believed nothing was impossible with God. I held on to that hope even in my sadness. My journey into understanding the depths of God's love and mercy for all men and women was on a trajectory course and I had much to learn. Jesus modeled his amazing love for us in his relationships with his followers. He accepted and loved those closest to him in spite of their weaknesses and sin, even Judas.

Ron was not asking me to change my views and he never gave any indication that he wanted to separate from his family. In one sense, our agreeing to disagree was freeing for both of us. Without his expressing these exact words, I believe Ron was asking me to listen to him and to be a part of his life. He felt being gay was his true self and he risked sharing that information with me, a family member. No wonder I sensed his relief in telling me and realized much later this was a major step in his officially "coming out" to a member of his family.

Several years earlier I had met some of Ron's friends but never any introductions to girlfriends. Stored somewhere in my memory bank was a conversation he'd shared with me in the early seventies while living in Portland, Oregon. He was working at Montgomery Ward and a female co-worker had asked him if he was gay. He'd told her no. I expressed surprise that she would ask him such a question just because he was single and living alone. A tiny seed was planted, but I'd forced it to the back of my mind.

Another memory surfaced. In 1972, we spent Thanksgiving in Newburg, Oregon, at our sister Dorothy's home. At that time, Ron was a student at Monmouth College of Education in Oregon. He'd lived in an off-campus apartment with three other guys—one engaged to be married. During one conversation we'd had that holiday, he'd told me about a lecture he had attended that described the lecturer's sex-change operation. I really didn't think much about it at the time, but put it in the category of another "exploratory college experience" that included listening to a variety of viewpoints.

Before finally falling asleep that memorable Christmas Eve, I decided to research homosexuality and convince Ron that this lifestyle was wrong. I had a plan. Little did I know at the time my emotionally painful but illuminating journey was well under way. My personal walk with God deepened over the years as I discovered how little I really understood about the depth of God's great mercy, grace and forgiveness.

On Christmas morning, no one suspected what had occurred the night before. Ron seemed even more relaxed. I now understand that Ron's "coming out" to me helped relieve some of his stress. Finally, someone he loved in his family knew his secret.

After that momentous Christmas, we returned to our home in Sun Valley, California while Ron returned to Portland. My research began. I read whatever information I could lay my hands on about homosexuality and stories of individuals who had turned away from the "gay lifestyle." At that time, "gay orientation" (used by the media and many writers today) was not part of the vocabulary used in my circles or in the limited reading I had done in this area. I searched my Bible for all references to homosexuality. I was convinced that if I just found the right article or essay and mailed it to Ron, he would see his error and want to change. Big sister Joyce was going to fix it! If someone had told me, "How naïve you are. You have much to learn," they would have been right. While processing and absorbing all the information Ron shared with me, I needed to continue living my life as wife, mother, and pastor's wife to our congregation. I began to wonder if there were others in our congregation, like me, who had "secrets" they were too embarrassed to share with anyone. My heart ached for Ron as I prayed and wondered again how homosexuality could have occurred in a Christian family. Aren't there guarantees in life that Christian families and individuals would be spared from experiencing such situations? I never remember anyone actually saying that but somehow I absorbed from my Christian community the idea that if we turn to Jesus, we won't experience such problems. I had not fully understood that Christians are *not* given a ticket that reads, "Exempt from . . ." but instead Jesus is *with* us through situations like these and his grace is sufficient.

In January of 1978, I saw an ad in *Christianity Today* that advertised a ministry to gays. The ad quoted a phrase from a Bible verse in I Corinthians 6:11, where the Apostle Paul wrote, "And that is what some of you were." The actual verses surrounding this phrase are found in 6:9–11 and are contained in a letter Paul wrote to a local church in Corinth. The city was a major commercial center and had a proud history of leadership in the Achaean League. It was the home of the temple of Aphrodite, and according to the ancient historian Strabo, was served by more than 1,000 pagan priestesses-prostitutes. The verses read:

> Do not be deceived: Neither the sexually immoral nor idolaters nor adulterers nor male prostitutes nor practicing homosexuals nor thieves nor the greedy nor drunkards nor slanderers nor swindlers will inherit the kingdom of God. *And that is what some of you were.* But you were washed, you were sanctified, you were justified in the name of the Lord Jesus Christ and by the Spirit of our God.

I decided to respond to the ad and ask for materials they would recommend I send Ron. I did not receive a response immediately so I impatiently went ahead and forwarded to Ron all the materials I had been collecting on my own. I meant well, but that was a mistake. A part of me believed that all one logically needed to change was to have the right information in front of them with a clear explanation that homosexual behavior was wrong and that settled it. I cringe at my lack of understanding in those early days. I just wanted to fix the situation and not have my life mixed up with these messy dilemmas. My personality bent is to relate to issues and life in an orderly and organized way. That way I could keep things under control. I didn't realize at the time this was my *modus operandi.* God was teaching me he is the only one who is really in control. He was not surprised in any way by what was going on in Ron's life and my family's life. I began to slowly understand that many of life's issues are surprisingly complex with no easy answers, even for Christian families. But through reading God's Word, I was reminded over and over again of the promise that he would never leave us or forsake us, even when our loved one tells us he or she is gay. I knew God loved Ron even if he experienced same sex attraction, but that did not mean this was God's intention for him to express his sexuality in this way. I know this is a hotly debated topic today with various opinions among Christians and non-Christians. I am grateful that today's Christian community has become much more open to discussing these issues than we were in the late seventies.

Finally, I heard from Pastor Tom, a member of the ministry I had written who explained he had been out of the country
and returned to a backlog of parish work that had prevented him
from writing me sooner. His letter was like water from a mountain
stream—sweet and refreshing. His phrases and insights are per-
manently imprinted on my brain. It was definitely a turning point
for me. I've included his letter in chapter 3.

Following my initial mailing to Ron, several months passed
before I received his response. He took the opportunity to mail me
questions most often asked about gays. He also stated he wondered
where I'd gotten my information, especially an article I'd included
titled "Homosexualism and Homosexuality." He felt it made some
gross generalizations. He wrote me in February 1978:

> Getting to know gay people, not just those who are hav-
> ing a hard time accepting themselves, can give a person
> more knowledge then any article or statistics . . . also it
> is the old school of thought that one is gay because of
> a dominant mother and/or a poor relationship with the
> father. This is true in some cases but not all people who
> have a dominant mother and/or a poor relationship with
> their father have gay tendencies. Some of my friends
> have had good relationships with their parents and are
> gay. Therefore I don't think that we can generalize about
> a gay person but must take each one as an individual.
> Many gay people who have accepted themselves are as
> happy as anyone else in society. The stigma of being gay
> has perpetuated the guilt feelings and low self-esteem
> that many gay people feel and go through. Please don't
> read between the lines in anything I have said. Just as you
> have said in your letter that you loved me and wanted
> me to know how you felt, I too love you and want you to
> know how I feel.

I was deeply grateful for Ron's letter and although he never
mentioned it, I sensed someone else had probably helped him
write it. His response did help to educate me that there is no "one"
root cause for homosexuality, and my earlier response to him, even
though sincere, had been simplistic and not fully developed. I was

on an intense learning curve and continued to pray for wisdom. My journey into real understanding and developing an informed point of view was ongoing. Through the years I began to read more articles on homosexuality and attempted to understand the homosexual community in light of Pastor Tom's observations. As Ron now shared with me information about his friends, his activities and experiences, I listened and was curious about his views and what shaped his thinking. I was no longer overwhelmed by this information but also continued to harbor sadness about Ron's future and wondered what lay ahead for him. As stories about AIDS began to dominate the news, I suspected Ron could be impacted by this. I wanted to be available for Ron and wanted him to see God's great love for him through me. Due to distance, we kept in touch by telephone with occasional out-of-state visits. The AIDS crisis actually brought us closer together as Ron reached out frequently to share his fears with me.

After Ron's Christmas Eve revelation, three years passed before my sisters and I had a conversation about this area of Ron's life, but by that time, they too, suspected Ron was gay. My parents did not know for many years. In fact, it was not until the mid-eighties, when Ron had full-blown AIDS that he told my parents.

Even when our family secret was finally revealed, my parents could not bring themselves to tell our aunts, uncles, and cousins that Ron was gay until he was severely ill. Later, my cousin told me they had long suspected this news about Ron but had never voiced their thoughts to my parents. Although they had little contact with Ron, I was extremely grateful for their friendliness and welcoming response when he attended family events.

There were awkward and yet humorous moments filled with foreboding during those intervening years. One incident occurred when Ron, my parents, and my sisters and I had gathered at my sister Dorothy's home. It was extremely warm in central California, and we were talking and having iced tea together. My mother loved iced tea. When we ran out of tea she picked up Ron's glass and drank from it while jokingly commenting, "It's okay. No one here has AIDS." At the time, we did not know the virus was already lurking in my brother's body, and would soon begin to manifest itself in disturbing ways. Shortly after that, my journey began to take another painful turn in the road. Before I describe that turning point, understanding my parents' background and our early years together as a family are important factors in Ron's story and my ongoing journey.

2

THE EARLY YEARS

WE WERE ELATED! FINALLY, a son and brother after three daughters. Ron was born June 12, 1951, in Whittier, California. My dad felt he had hit the jackpot. Our baby brother captured our hearts, and we affectionately called him Ronnie. He was a picture-postcard baby, with lots of dark hair, blue eyes, and a winsome smile. Over the years, he was the recipient of our love and endured our good-natured sisterly teasing. At his birth, Dorothy was nine years old, Karon six, and I was the eight-year-old middle sister. Our aunts and uncles, who only had daughters, celebrated the news with us that finally a boy was born into the Smith household to carry on the family name.

As I thought through our family dynamics in an attempt to understand all the issues my family faced over the years, I found myself going back and rehearsing in my mind what I knew about my parents' background and their developmental years.

During the first years of their marriage my parents, Ray and Doris Smith, scratched out a poor, hardscrabble existence on a small farm not far from Robstown, Texas. With three little girls in tow, they soon became managers of a local laundry after the end of World War II.

In 1947, they dreamed about farming a small plot of land in the San Joaquin Valley of central California. They piled all their belongings into the car and squeezed my sisters and me into the backseat. They drove through the deserts of New Mexico and Arizona in search of a new beginning. Dad's love affair with California had started when the Navy stationed him in San Diego for basic training. Most of Dad's brothers and sisters had already made their way out west shortly after the war ended so my parents decided to follow.

Like many others following WWII, they thought California was the land of milk and honey where all their dreams would come true. But, those dreams cost a lot of money they did not have. After living in California for a year in a small trailer and no job in sight, they packed their bags and prepared to move back to Texas. The night before they were to leave, my dad was offered a job as a plumber's helper with the promise that he could learn the plumbing trade and eventually qualify as a journeyman. Little did my parents know this decision would forever change our lives economically and spiritually. As I reflect on my parents' life experiences during their youth, I realize how their difficult experiences shaped them and later shaped me and my siblings.

It's not surprising to know that growing up with a dad who endured significant loss in his childhood meant there would be ramifications impacting our family life. It wasn't until many years had passed before I began to understand the degree of deprivation my dad experienced as a child—emotionally and physically. I believe his inability to nurture and his lack of healthy parenting skills were all related to his own difficult childhood. It took years of maturing on my part and becoming a parent before I began to extend more grace to my dad and soften some of my criticisms. Dad grew up in poverty in south Texas with little education. One of ten children, he was born in 1918, a twin to my Aunt Fay. When his mother died of pneumonia she left behind her husband, a baby, one set of two-year-old twins and six other children ranging in age from four to 16 years old. She had already buried one baby. After 21 years of living in poverty and birthing 10 children, she was 38 years-old when she died. Life was hard in rural Texas. There were no modern conveniences in their small house—no indoor plumbing, no electricity, and no running water. That would come later. The Depression years were just around the corner, but it was already difficult to operate a small farm and feed a large family in the early 1920s. Dad told us how his sisters and brothers filled their stomachs with mounds of pinto beans and cornbread to stave off their hunger. He especially came to love cornbread dipped in buttermilk and eaten with pickled pigs' feet. As a child, I screwed up my face and almost gagged when Dad would eat his favorite evening snack. I only needed to try it once.

I learned that my grandfather had been a harsh man who did not tolerate any nonsense and freely disciplined with the belt. My dad's stories filled me with dread and some fear. Dad was never reluctant to use the belt on my siblings and me. My aunts shared with my mother one of the reasons they married young, and to the wrong men, was to escape home and their "mean father." I never met him, as he died in 1939 in a car accident—hit by a drunk driver shortly before my parents were married. Photographs portray him with a dour countenance and stern demeanor. I've often wondered what it would have been like to know him. Had poverty, hard times, and so many mouths to feed sucked the joy of living from his life? I live with many unanswered questions about my paternal grandparents as Dad rarely talked about his parents or how he felt growing up in such poverty. It was difficult for him to speak about feelings. On a vacation trip to Texas from California I was so excited about seeing my maternal grandparents and as we were driving in the car I said excitedly, "This is like a dream that is finally coming true." My dad responded sharply, "We don't talk like that." I was hurt and wondered what I had said that caused such a harsh response. As far as I knew, Dad never received spiritual instruction or guidance from his family.

By the time he finished fourth grade, he was needed to pick cotton under the broiling sun in the cotton fields of Texas. His older brothers and his father convinced him that if he quit school he could be a "man" and work the fields along with them. Years later my mother told me this was a decision he bitterly regretted. He discovered what hard work meant at a very early age. His father remarried after the death of my grandmother, and two more half-brothers and a half-sister were added to the family. Dad never felt close to his stepmother. At the height of the Depression my grandfather was feeding 22 people at his table three times a day. A farm-style homemade table with two long benches on either side seated everyone. Adding to the difficulties of the times, Dad's oldest sister, Lena, returned home with three small children after her husband's desertion. My grandfather would not tolerate anyone questioning his authority, even his adult children. The story is told that when my Aunt Lena stood up to him he slapped her face in front of the entire family.

During my elementary years, it seemed like we had an abundance of gifts at Christmas. It was at this time Dad would reminisce about his Christmases as a child. They were painful memories. All he received was an orange and some hard candy. Being so young, sadness and pity flooded my heart as I thought how awful it must have been for him not to have any Christmas presents. Those years of extreme poverty, backbreaking work, and lack of nurturing marked my dad for life.

My mother Doris Koch was born in Texas in 1922, to a loving family with German immigrant roots. My maternal grandparents had a small farm that met their needs and eventually brought some profit to them. Grandma Koch was Catholic, and Grandpa was Lutheran. The children were raised Catholic; Grandpa continued attending the Lutheran Church with occasional special visits to the local Catholic parish. My mother was one of four children, with only three of them surviving childhood. Her family knew tragedy. My grandparents experienced the death of their oldest son when he was four years-old. Their youngest child, Olga Mae, was delivered at home by a doctor who was drunk during the delivery. After a very difficult birth, he set her aside as dead. The Mammy who helped said, "That baby ain't dead," and she had my aunt breathing after 15 minutes had elapsed. Consequently, dear Olga Mae lived the rest of her life mentally challenged and epileptic due to oxygen deprivation to her brain.

In 1939, my blonde haired, blue-eyed 17 year-old mother met Ray Smith at a dance in little Tynan, Texas, and immediately fell in love. She dropped out of high school with one year to complete, and they were married in 1940. They began 66 years of married life until Dad's death in 2005. My sisters and I were born in rapid succession. With three dependents, Dad was not drafted into World War II until early 1945, when the Navy finally "invited" him to join them in the Philippines for the remaining six months of the war.

A dramatic event changed all our lives in 1950. At the invitation of my dad's older brother, Mom and Dad visited the Christian Church in El Monte, California. An older couple in the church began to visit my parents' home and regularly shared with them what it meant to have a personal relationship with Jesus Christ. Even though my mother identified herself as Catholic, her faith was more habitual than heartfelt. My parents were born again and were baptized. Mom found this couple's kindness to them irresistible. No doubt their friendliness and concern filled a gap in their young lives as they settled into living in California away from family in Texas. My Catholic grandmother was disappointed that her daughter had become a Protestant. My sisters and I—ten, eight, and six years old at the time—soon followed in our parents' steps and were baptized. Dad did not speak a great deal about this turning point in his life, but he became a faithful church attendee and made sure that we also attended church. God, in His mercy and grace, reached out and touched my dad's heart. His personality did not totally change, but he did have a new focus and desire to know God and his Word, the Bible. Prayer before meals became a part of our lives. Dad seemed to change when he prayed and would speak in a tender tone we did not hear often, and with each prayer he always asked God to forgive him for his sins. Dad's harsh upbringing and little education seemed to limit his ability to express verbally his emotions and feelings.

With the birth of my brother Ron in 1951, and our family complete, Dad was well on his way to becoming a plumbing contractor and eventually owning a successful plumbing business. He worked hard learning the plumbing trade while trying to provide for his family. Like many men of his generation, he didn't know how to play with children easily, nurture them, dream with them about the future, or praise and encourage them. He didn't want to spoil his children. Dad's love for us was exhibited by his providing shelter, food, and clothing for his family. Over the years, I began to appreciate more and more Dad's strong work ethic, his commitment to our family and his love for my mother. At times, Dad's resentment over his impoverished past revealed itself through his lack of trust in others and his fear he would be taken advantage of in business because he lacked an education. His distrust and anger would sometimes spill over in his interactions and treatment of store clerks, insurance salesmen, and doctors.

Because Dad worked so hard, he had little time for games or other activities with us children, and any discipline issues were resolved with the belt. Today, we would call them beatings. In spite of the deprivations Dad experienced in his childhood, he was growing in his faith and beginning to find some financial success compared to his earlier years. He felt honored to serve on church boards but was also very critical of people and decisions with which he disagreed.

Into these family dynamics, Ron was born. I loved playing with him as a baby and I was thankful I had a brother. I played the role of big sister and babysitter along with Dorothy and Karon. On occasion, my sisters and I would tease him to the point of tears. I remember Karon and I hosting a slumber party at our home and we thought it would be great fun to scare our little brother by sneaking outside, making noises and scraping our fingers along his bedroom window. Just as we were doing this his window shade flew up with a bang and he started howling. We burst out laughing—goal achieved. Later, when I saw how frightened he was, I did feel remorse for our actions and, of course, my mother was very unhappy with us.

As a young child, Ron's countenance was usually very serious. When I look at family pictures, I sometimes see fear in his eyes—fear he would make a mistake and get into trouble. I was too young to understand why at the time. When encouraging Ron to join the local Little League team, Mom asked Dad to teach him how to throw a ball and swing a bat, but it was torture for Ron. On the rare occasions this happened, he could never throw the ball the way Dad wanted. Dad would grow impatient, yell, and verbally assault him. This was not a fun activity or bonding time for either one of them.

When Ron was in elementary school and junior high, my mom asked Dad to take Ron with him on some of his plumbing calls. Ron would come home in tears from these experiences, saying he never wanted to go again because Dad wouldn't talk to him. When Mom reproached Dad for this, his heartbreaking response was, "What do you talk to a kid about?" Dad didn't know how to be a Dad. All he knew was hard work beginning at a very young age. Even though his own father had been extremely harsh, my mother told me Dad always respected him. Unable to express his deepest emotions, I believe my dad longed for a loving relationship with his father.

While all of this was occurring, our church continued to be very important in the life of our family. By this time, my sisters and I participated in all the youth activities sponsored by Brea First Baptist. Ron followed in our footsteps and professed faith in Jesus and was baptized. He, too, later became active in our church's youth group.

As Ron and I grew closer over the years, we became more open with each other. We shared at a deeper level than ever before, and he talked to me about some of the fears he experienced as a child. I discovered he had developed a distorted understanding of God that could only be described as dysfunctional. I did not understand everything that was happening with Ron when we were younger. I only observed behavior I could not explain. Ron developed an irrational fear that God would take his mother away unless he was a "good boy." He pictured God as a father with a big "stick" who used that stick whenever you did anything that displeased him. He went around our home and in his school classroom with a fake smile on his face. He saw God as a tyrant who was difficult to please. During Ron's fourth grade year, his teacher made a home visit and shared with my parents what she and the school principal had observed about Ron's unusual behavior in the classroom. She told them Ron was not a troublemaker but a troubled child. He had an unusual smile all the time. His demeanor was tense, fearful, and his social interactions with others immature. Though I did not sit in on the meeting, my parents later shared bits and pieces of the conversation with my sisters and me.

His teacher suggested my parents consider counseling for Ron, but Mom and Dad were reluctant to pursue this course of action and thought it was unnecessary. Instead, they decided they would be able to talk Ron out of his fears. They were embarrassed, and in their minds only "people who were crazy sought counseling," a view that many people held in the late fifties and early sixties. Trying to step back into my parent's thinking at the time, I am sure they did not understand the consequences of not getting professional counseling for Ron. Psychology was not a field they were familiar with and I doubt if they personally knew anyone at that time who had received counseling. Ron's issue did not seem that serious to them and they truly believed one could be talked out of their fears.

Ron was thirteen when I left home and married. I was in and out of the house during my college years while Ron was entering puberty. Ron was nine when Dorothy married and 11 years old when Karon married. I was self-absorbed with my own life during those years. I did not pay a lot of attention to Ron even though I loved him and felt a desire to protect him. During my sophomore year of college we grew even closer. When I was home for the summer and school vacations we played board games together and traveled to Texas for a visit with my maternal grandparents. Because we were the only siblings still living at home, I remember our laughing and talking together but I cannot recall any in depth conversations about what he was feeling or experiencing. Dorothy and her husband had moved to Thailand in 1964 as missionaries and were gone for four years—another loss for Ron. When I began to plan my wedding my mother told me that Ron really wanted to have some part in it. I was touched by his request and asked him to be a candle lighter along with my former college roommate. He was pleased that he could be involved in some specific way.

As I look back now, it feels like our conversations revolved around "surface" issues and not life issues that really mattered. We didn't discuss his feelings and he did not reveal to me that he often felt alone. Some years after Ron told me he was gay, he admitted that he struggled psychologically as a teenager and kept his true feelings hidden because he was afraid of what he was experiencing. He didn't know who to talk to about what was happening to him. It was uncomfortable talking about emotions and fears in our home. It was not a pattern our parents had modelled for us because it had not been modelled for them.

Ron was very attached to our mother but that did not worry me. As a child he was possessive with his toys, and I remember thinking he did not share very well when neighborhood children were over to play, but that was not unusual but really typical of so many children. My husband and I moved out-of-state in 1966 so my contact with Ron became even more limited during his high school years except for holiday visits or an occasional visit to Oregon. When we moved back to California in 1973, Ron was 22 years old and we enjoyed being together whenever we could but it was limited. We always felt a certain measure of trust with each other and we shared similar views on a variety of topics.

Ron was shy and considered by some to be "the quiet type." He was definitely not an extrovert. Ron's blue eyes engaged his listeners and his smile was genuine and I felt he conveyed warmth and friendliness. He was not a voracious reader but did enjoy an occasional good read. Most of all he enjoyed listening to music, watching TV, movies and travel.

As he matured, I saw in Ron a compassionate heart that cared about injustice in the United States and around the world. During the Viet Nam war era, he was adamant about not going to war and opposed US policy in Viet Nam. He sought Conscientious Objector status and gathered all the papers and references required for submission. My husband wrote a letter confirming Ron's pacifist position was longstanding and not something newly developed. He was denied CO status but instead was granted deferred status. We were all relieved.

After Ron's death, I discovered an intimate and revealing timeline he had written when he was in rehabilitation for his alcoholism. As part of the process of wanting to better understand and help Ron, apparently one of the counselors at the rehabilitation center asked him to write a sequential record of memorable events in his life. I found this very difficult to read, but it also opened my eyes to some of Ron's deepest struggles. Through my tears, I read about a young man who at 13 felt abandoned when I married and left home and there were no more sisters around. My parents were very active in the fraternal organizations known as the Masonic Lodge and Eastern Star. As I went away to college, they became more involved with these organizations and spent two to three nights a week away from home. It never occurred to them how lonely Ron felt during that time. He went on to write about finding liquor my parents had stored in their home, and after drinking all alone one evening he describes getting drunk for the first time and becoming very sick.

I went on to read that at the age of three he remembered being labeled a "mama's boy," and later being afraid to go to kindergarten. He wrote that he wondered *What if something happened to Mom? What if she died while I'm gone?* He indicated it was difficult for him to concentrate during his elementary years, that he daydreamed often, and went around always saying, "I'm sorry, I'm sorry" (for who he was?). He referenced being slow to develop, feeling behind other students, unsure, not keeping up with his school work, and seeing himself as being "different." He went on to write how religious his family was and how he started to learn from the church about heaven, hell, and death to the sinner! He ended that entry with, "I was afraid to die (didn't know if I was good or bad)."

In another entry he described feeling guilty over masturbating when he was around 11 or 12 years old. He added he had no male guidance. The counselor noted on the timeline a statement Ron had made to him: "Concerned about not having enough contact with males." At 13, he admitted to having his first homosexual encounter but did not describe the experience or the circumstances. He added he began to smoke marijuana when he was 16 and after that occasionally used what he called "recreational drugs" until he was 34. Ron writes he had his second gay experience at age 21 and when he was 23 entered a relationship that lasted four years. He started drinking vodka and scotch heavily at this time, thinking it was just part of the lifestyle. At 25, he discovered his partner had given him his first case of venereal disease. He writes that he was monogamous and this discovery made him feel alone, hurt, and angry. Frequent arguments led to their eventually breaking off the relationship.

At 27, Ron wanted to escape from his job in sales, and he was unhappy. He decided to travel to Europe for three months visiting friends and touring on his own while pursuing his lifelong dream of travel. On his timeline he wrote that he smoked hash a lot while traveling and survived on bread and cheese to save money. When he returned from Europe, he settled in San Francisco for several years and thought that he would get closer to his family by living in state. He later admitted that his worst mistake was moving to San Francisco. It was there he believed he became infected with the AIDS virus.

Before Ron was aware he was HIV positive, he began to experience health problems. As his drinking, drug usage and sexual activity increased in the late seventies and early eighties, one of the consequences he experienced was health issues with his liver. For three months he struggled with liver problems and finally a biopsy and tests revealed he had Hepatitis. A treatment regimen eventually brought him relief. He moved back to Oregon during this time and held various jobs in sales and later became a produce manager in a family-owned grocery business.

I was shocked as I read his timeline and discovered how deeply he was involved with what he labeled "recreational" drugs. He even named them: acid, coke, mescaline, crystal meth, and speed. Reading this helped me to understand why I received such strange phone calls from him over the years. At 30, he entered into another four-year relationship, but his use of alcohol damaged that relationship also. When he was 34 years old he entered his first treatment center for alcoholism due to his increasing paranoia and insecurity. Ron wrote that his partner blamed him for their break-up because of his heavy drinking. Friends told him he was verbally abusive when drinking, and he experienced blackouts and could not make it into work. Ron walked out of the treatment center after completing 29 days of the 30 day plan. He said, "I must not have been ready. I was drinking again in three weeks." I knew Ron had entered a treatment program and we spoke often over the phone while he was there, but he had not revealed any of these details to me at the time. One of my sad regrets for Ron is that he felt too embarrassed to discuss his struggles and fears with anyone as a child or as a teenager. He hid his fears and difficulties from our parents, teachers, his pastor, and various youth leaders. In his thinking, there was no one in whom he could confide. No one he felt safe enough to share his deepest thoughts and experiences. Reading these handwritten comments filled me with agony. My mind was flooded with unanswered questions. *How had I failed him? What could we have done to provide a safe and secure place for Ron to grow and develop?* There were so many important life issues rarely discussed in our home—emotions, dreams, struggles—questions about life and sex, and why Ron felt different from others. My heart still aches when I think of his loneliness. I wondered what had blocked his ability to know and trust in God's deep love?

In Henri Nouwen's book, *The Inner Voice of Love,* I can hear his emotional pain as he describes his own personal struggles with acceptance, fear, rejection, feeling forgotten, misunderstood, and his desire to be loved. I see in Ron's life echoes of these same emotions. More questions filled my mind as I tried to understand why Ron apparently could not feel or experience God's overwhelming love for him. Nouwen writes:

> God says to you, I love you, I am with you, I want to see
> you come closer to me and experience the joy and peace

of my presence. I want to give you a new heart and a new spirit ... All that is mine is yours. Just trust me and let me be your God. This is the voice to listen to. And that listening requires a real choice, not just once in a while but every moment of each day and night. It is you who decides what you think, say, and do. You can think yourself into a depression, you can talk yourself into low self-esteem, and you can act in a self-rejecting way. But you always have a choice to think, speak, and act in the name of God and so move toward the Light, the Truth, and the Life.[1]

Nouwen strongly believes in the individual's personal responsibility to choose what one thinks and does. He writes about this because he, too, struggled with making wise choices.

Throughout Ron's life his emotional pain, life experiences, and alcoholism seemed to drown out his ability to hear this redemptive voice, thus he chose not to listen. There were fleeting moments in his life when he experienced joy, felt confident and accepted, but sadly, they were few.

1 Nouwen, *Inner Voice*, 113–114.

3

THE TURNING POINT

I EAGERLY OPENED THE letter from Pastor Tom. Like a thirsty sponge, I soaked up his words of wisdom, comfort, hope, and understanding. Emotionally, I was thrilled and saddened. I returned to his letter often as Ron's downward spiral began. His words lifted the burden I felt about how to best articulate my belief to Ron. I wanted Ron to understand why he did not have to live a gay lifestyle. I lived with the common evangelical idea that if I could quote just the right Scripture, Ron would understand and want to change. I fell into the trap of thinking that his eternal destiny was in my hands and I was responsible for explaining my belief so clearly he couldn't help but understand and be transformed. Yes, my words mattered, but I assumed more responsibility than God intended for me. He is the author of salvation and repentance, not me. Ultimately it is the Spirit of God working in the heart and mind of each individual that gives the power to become a new creation in Christ Jesus (I Cor 5:17).

As I pulled out Pastor Tom's letter once again, his words filled me with hope and reminded me of my role as Ron's sister. Here's the full text of his response to my letter.

January 28, 1978

Dear Joyce:

Holy Greetings in the wonderful Name of JESUS! Thanks for your letter of January 4th. Sorry to have been so long in getting back to you. I have had quite a load of mail of late, plus parish work and then preparing to go on mission to Europe in a few more days, which takes me away until well into the summer. Therefore, I am replying now before any more time goes by and then I would be away and out of contact all during those months.

To your letter: Frankly, I believe that you handled Ron in about the best way that you could have. One thing he does not need at this point, especially if he is getting into addicting habits, which will only cause to depress him, is to have someone go on the Anita Bryant kick. The articles you may think about sending him that would take it from your point of view (if your point of view is something that would ever cause him more condemnation) would be useless. I am sure that if he has had the same background you have, he is already only too well aware of the whole line. The fact that he has chosen to believe certain parts of the Bible and to reject others tells you already that he is believing a lie and has chosen to do so. It sounds to me as though he is finally at the peak of his homosexuality but remember that he never asked to be homosexual. The battle still rages in Christian and non-Christian circles about whether or not people are born homosexual. I won't get into it because I am not sure either way. However, I do not believe that people necessarily choose to be homosexual. If they knew what it was like, they would not choose it. Hammering them with Bible verses only makes things worse because it alienates them from the only source of real help and deliverance, Jesus Christ Himself. After all, if the physician condemns the patient for being sick and the physician is the only one who is able to bring about the cure . . .?! In this case, it is not the Physician who is condemning the person, but His assistants. Either way, you cannot clean a fish until you have caught it and such it is with Ron. The fact that he thought enough of you to tell you says a lot and the fact that he went back to Portland probably not sorry he told you is positive because he has now "come out" to you, someone whom he loves. You have got to keep the door open to him until he is able to discern the difference between the Holy Spirit convicting him of sin and that which it is often confused with—guilt. The difference between guilt and condemnation is conviction. Only the latter comes from God the Holy Spirit.

His sin is not his homosexuality; that is only the outward manifestation of his inward condition. If you can reach his will, regardless of what his sin outwardly appears to be, you will have it. God always looks on the heart and that is where you should aim. If he comes out of this, it will be because he was loved as a person, not tolerated by the religious. Keep that line of communication open, even to the point of never mentioning it. Let him bring it up. Then you are not forever talking about the same old subject, but he can enjoy a relationship with you that the world cannot give him, especially the gay world. Even if he seems to be going miles in that direction and away from you (like, if he were to find some "Mr. Right" and they lived together, etc., for some time and Ron's spirits seemed so much better for a bit, it is only short-lived and be ready for the crash that will inevitably come).

There is little else I can say at this point. If I were you though I would not bring up the subject, nor send him any material. Otherwise you are forever reminding him he is a homosexual and you know it and he is ceasing to be your brother, purely and simply. Keep in mind also that his sin is not very much different than ours—it still starts in the heart, etc. The outward expression of it is the difference and with Ron it happens to be something that is so socially unacceptable that we tend to make it worse than what it really is, hence estranging ourselves from the person who is caught in that expression of their sin nature. Of course, out of self-defense, the gay person and the gay society flock together and build up a whole sub-culture around it and try to make it respectable. Even if it never becomes respectable, it is still a sub-culture and gives Ron some lifestyle he can grab onto just to feel as though he can find a niche somewhere.

I hope I am coming through . . . I don't know. But, if Ron would like to write me some time, I would be open to the idea. As I said, I will be away for some months to do some ministering in Europe, but any letters that arrive my secretary will hold until my return. Blessings.

Yours for Calvary,
Pastor Tom
Psalm 27:4

Pastor Tom's letter freed me from the false burden of believing I could transform Ron's life with the right article or the right combination of words. I had forgotten that God could use any means to teach truth and transform a life. That did not excuse me from being a voice for biblical truth at appropriate times but I sensed that loving Ron was the most important thing I could do.

Because of Pastor Tom's experience, I believed he was a man who understood Ron's real need and he helped me to see that his homosexuality did not have to separate us. I could trust God to speak to Ron's heartfelt need and continue to love him unconditionally. My relationship with Ron began to focus more on him and loving him well. I didn't have to be concerned about not bringing up the subject of homosexuality—Ron always did. I found he often discussed it with me and soon began to tell me about his broken relationships.

Ron had many questions about God, being gay, dealing with fear, death, and the dying process. He believed the God he loved made him gay. I thought it was interesting that he frequently used the phrase "the God I love," suggesting, I believe, that he worshiped a different God than the one I worshipped. It seemed to me that this type of thinking allowed him to rationalize responsibility for his behavior because "God made me this way." This may not have been a conscious thought but one that perhaps was buried deep within his subconscious.

Ron occasionally attended various churches and one time proudly told me he met a lesbian couple on staff at a Methodist church and they visited him in his home. During this time of searching for answers, he even referenced a séance he attended— evidence to me that his desire for inner peace was so strong he was willing to try anything. Over the years we continued to carry on long conversations in person and over the telephone about all of these subjects and more.

Reading Pastor Tom's letter again after all these years, still fills me with admiration. His understanding, foresight, and almost prophetic view of Ron's downward spiral unless he yielded his mind and heart to the one who could bring him forgiveness, healing, and wholeness was profoundly insightful.

Late in 1978, Ron moved to San Francisco for several years. Unknown to him, and most people at that time, was the startling news that the AIDS virus was spreading in San Francisco and many men were developing a pattern of illness that baffled the medical community. In June 1981, the first AIDS (Acquired Immunodeficiency Syndrome) cases and deaths were reported in the United States. According to the Center for Disease Control, the number of cases and deaths among persons with AIDS increased rapidly during the 1980s. The media reported alarming stories about the possible contamination of the nation's blood supply. Nearly all cases of HIV due to blood transfusions occurred before the national screening of the blood supply was in place in 1985. Ryan White of Kokomo, Indiana, became the face of fear that gripped many cities in our nation as he contracted the HIV virus through a blood transfusion to treat his hemophilia. At the age of 13, he received his AIDS diagnosis. He died in 1990 due to a respiratory infection, a complication of AIDS. The media continued to publish stories of gay men becoming gravely ill and dying. Fear was rampant in the gay community. Ron was no exception.

One evening I answered my phone and listened while Ron's sobs echoed across the telephone line as he debated whether or not he should be tested for HIV. I encouraged him to take the test, but he was distraught and afraid. Many of our long phone conversations focused on whether or not he should be tested. Fear paralyzed him. He continued to self-medicate with alcohol and drugs even while meeting with a counselor. Emotionally he was unstable. His counselor encouraged him not to self-medicate, offering to help him with an alternative drug that would ease his emotional pain but make him ill if he drank. At first he agreed to pursue this course of therapy but later stopped. His search for help included contacts with the Church of Religious Science as well as attempts at meditation and relaxation techniques.

Throughout this time, I continued to encourage Ron to be tested. After all, if he tested negative, what a relief for him. If he tested positive, he could immediately begin a regimen of medication. It took two tortured years before Ron had the courage to go ahead with the test. At the time, I thought I was being helpful to Ron by objectively explaining his options to him, but psychologically and emotionally Ron felt as if he were playing a game of tag with a death sentence. I had not fully grasped the significance of what he was experiencing.

He knew of friends who had developed carcinomas, thrush, dementia, and various other opportunistic infections. Would these infections now become a part of his daily life? He told me it wasn't death he feared so much but the process of dying. Daily he checked the obituaries in the newspaper to find the names of friends who had died.

One cloudy November day, I received his tearful telephone call. "Joyce, I'm positive." Through shared tears, I tried to comfort him and give him hope. I encouraged him to contact his counselor who was in Portland, unlike me far-away in Indiana. His counselor could guide him to the resources available to help him cope with what it would be like to live with AIDS.

During those days when he was coming to terms with his diagnosis, one particular phone call frightened me. I was in my office when Ron called threatening suicide. My heart sank. Numerous panic-stricken phone calls followed. I put him in touch with a ministry to gays located in Seattle, Washington, called Metanoia, which means "repentance" in Greek. During that time period, his phone calls were often bizarre. I was deeply concerned for him and prayed someone from this ministry could reach his heart and mind.

In spite of his diagnosis, Ron remained committed to the gay community even though he told me he was celibate. He eventually made contact with Metanoia and spoke with one of their counselors. Later, Ron angrily told me he believed the counselor was a traitor to *who he really was* because he admitted to having lived a gay lifestyle previously but no longer. I was startled by Ron's vehement attitude towards this man. Disappointment flooded my mind and heart with Ron's negative response. I was looking for the magic bullet that would change everything for him. My tearful prayers were filled with pleas for healing and protection for Ron. What was going to happen to him? I wanted him to know God truly loved him and could meet his need right where he was. My journey involved learning how to trust the Holy Spirit to transform Ron's life and that I could not "fix it." I needed to be a loving sister who was not always preaching to him what he already knew, but instead a sister he could trust and respect; one who was willing and open to talking about his life whenever he brought up the subject of being gay, which was often. He continued to believe that God created him with a gay orientation and refused to acknowledge that homosexual acts were wrong.

I longed for the day when Ron would declare God had miraculously turned around his life and his sexual orientation. I imagined him traveling and sharing his testimony of victory. That was not happening. As the years went by, I continued to remind myself that homosexuality is symptomatic of deeper underlying issues and needs. I thought I knew what they were but soon realized I was only scratching the surface. We are far more complicated human beings than I understood. I was focused on external symptoms and not what Ron's deep internal needs were. Pastor Tom's counsel became more meaningful to me as I sought to understand the dynamic surrounding homosexuality and how I might respond with deeper insight into what I was discovering.

The most helpful insights that aided me in my attempt to clarify my thinking and create a meaningful relationship with Ron centered on three major concepts Pastor Tom brought to light.

1) *Causing someone like Ron to feel more condemnation than what they already feel would be useless.* When Jesus responded to the Pharisees in Luke 5:31 who complained about his eating and drinking with tax collectors and sinners, he said, "It is not the healthy who need a doctor, but the sick. I have not come to call the righteous, but sinners to repentance." I realized once again I did not need to heap upon Ron Bible verse after Bible verse but to listen to him and let Jesus' love for him flow through me.

2) *Rarely, if ever, does a man or woman choose their sexual orientation.* Acting upon one's homosexual orientation outside of biblical teaching is where a follower of Jesus Christ must make a decision. Either to live in obedience to Scripture and forego any lifestyle that gives in to disordered desires, including immoral heterosexual behavior, or to reinterpret what God's Word says about immorality and live outside the boundaries of God's moral law. As I pondered the counsel from Pastor Tom, I was startled to realize he had written what my mind and heart had been weighing regarding my relationship with Ron and what it might look like going forward. He helped me to understand that no one, or at least very few, "choose" to be gay. I came to realize the crux of the issue is whether one chooses to act on those inclinations by engaging in homosexual behavior.

3) *His sin is not his homosexuality; that is only the outward manifestation of his inward condition. God always looks on the heart and that is where you should aim.* This view of how sin manifests itself is applicable for all of us. It really does begin in the heart and our behavior reveals who we are and what we think in our inmost being. In response to criticism the Pharisees aimed at Jesus regarding his disciples not washing their hands before they ate, he gave them a parable and

then interpreted it to his disciples. In Matthew 15:1–20 this encounter is revealed in detail. In particular, Jesus tells his disciples, "Don't you see that whatever enters the mouth goes into the stomach and then out of the body? *But the things that come out of the mouth come from the heart, and these defile you.* For out of the heart come evil thoughts, murder, adultery, sexual immorality, theft, false testimony, slander. These are what defile you; but eating with unwashed hands does not defile you."

Through my experience with Ron and hearing the stories of men and women who found themselves struggling with same sex attraction—an attraction they did not choose and that frightens them—I have a better understanding of the emotional trauma many feel. Initially, I had no understanding of what it would be like for someone to think they might be gay. I never considered that young adolescents could experience same sex attraction, let alone struggle with why they were experiencing these emotions. However, as the years went by and my reading broadened, I wept as I began to understand how devastating and confusing these feelings were, especially for Christian young people. I reflected on times when I had observed Ron appearing to be unusually nervous and anxious; never associating it with fears that he had a gay orientation. I noticed this type of behavior even more in his late adolescence and as a young adult in Portland. I couldn't understand why he often seemed to be anxious and felt it was just a personality tendency that would change if he made more friends. As a result of Pastor Tom's letter and further reading, my knowledge base and attitude toward those struggling with a gay orientation was undergoing change. Many young men and women are shocked and frightened in early adolescence when they begin to experience uninvited emotions and feelings.

My compassion for Ron and desire to be available for him no matter what continued to grow as my understanding increased. The long difficult phone calls that became a part of our relationship were important to me in spite of their being very uncomfortable at times. Not only was God working in Ron's life, but he was working in mine, allowing me to come alongside someone I loved—someone who really needed to know God's great love.

As a young person, I rarely thought about homosexuality and was not aware that individuals experienced feelings they never asked for. My Christian world was narrow and I honestly could not say I personally knew anyone who was openly gay. My only prior experience in this area had been what I observed in movies or learned in books.

One particular incident stands out in my mind during my college freshman year when I was enrolled in a General Psychology class. My professor admitted to us that his most difficult counseling cases were with homosexuals and he found their behavior disgusting. That was the prevailing view held by many Christians in my circles at that time. This was part of my evangelical milieu. Intellectually I knew that *God so loved the world,* but I thought individuals who were steeped in sinful acts had to change their lives before they could genuinely be found acceptable in the eyes of God. As I became more aware of Ron's struggles, it became personal; not something that was happening to "the other." Homosexuality and AIDS were now a part of my life, and my family's life, and always would be. This realization hit me clearly in the face as I began to observe and understand the inner turmoil and personal pain someone I loved was experiencing. It was no longer an issue "out there" but this was an issue in my world. My journey became more difficult because grieving for my brother and his AIDS diagnosis was now a part of my life I could not change. However, my love for my brother never changed. Other things about me began to change. I no longer felt embarrassed or the need to hide the fact my brother was gay. I did not want to isolate myself or withdraw from someone I thought might be gay. Whenever I encountered an individual who was struggling over a loved one's gay lifestyle, I immediately wanted to reach out and tell that person, "I understand what you're going through. I've been there too. You are not alone."

Over time I began to meet some of Ron's friends and I found myself enjoying their company, but also curious about their background and wondering what personal struggles they experienced as they became aware of their same sex attraction. As I encountered clerks, waiters, and people I met at conferences who I thought might be gay or they told me they were, I found myself deliberately engaging in conversations with them because in one sense, I wanted to make up for the times when Ron felt he was mistreated by others. The responses I received were always positive.

In the early nineties, when my husband and I were visiting Ron's home in Portland, a neighbor from down the street stopped by to see him. His neighbor was another gay man who had AIDS, was on disability, and had his caregiver with him. Bob was in his late thirties or early forties. He rambled in his speech and as I walked into another part of the house, I heard him ask why people hated him so much. I was startled that he was sharing his feelings so openly and it was probably due to the disease breaking down some of his social inhibitions. I heard him say, "I never hurt anyone. Why won't people accept me? Why do I have to have AIDS? Why do I have to die?" His caregiver was trying to get him to be quiet and calm down, but I felt emotionally wrenched as I heard this man express the anguish he was feeling deep within himself. I could tell it was upsetting to Ron as he became very quiet and his face took on a pained sorrowful expression. Bob was disturbed and only wanted to talk about his physical condition but I also heard his cry for understanding. Silently I prayed for him. God was allowing me to experience and see up close the deadly face of AIDS and its consequences. I wondered, "Was this preparation for what I would see happen to Ron in the future?"

These events certainly impacted my thinking and were like rungs on a ladder. Each event, each encounter with Ron, each book I read served to educate me and heighten my sensitivity toward those who were struggling with their sexuality and those who seemed to embrace it.

From very little knowledge about homosexuality in the early days of the 1970s until today, I continue to be on a steep learning curve. That learning curve included many one on one conversations initiated by Ron about his gay lifestyle. It also included reading numerous articles and books while learning about the worldwide rise of AIDS and its devastating impact. My learning curve heightened even more as I began to write the story of my journey with Ron. My reading list continued to grow and I found myself overwhelmed with all that was available to read. There were days when I had to set aside my reading as my sadness deepened. I was processing so much emotional information I soon realized I had to find a balance and take occasional breaks from focusing only on books dealing with this topic. Out of that reading, I developed a reading list that can be found at the back of the book. It is not exhaustive, but would be helpful for the Christian seeking to increase their understanding.

In 2011 I read Mel White's story, *Stranger at the Gate,* one of the most emotionally painful books I encountered. Mel describes growing up in an evangelical and fundamentalist home, trying to figure out why he was attracted to the same sex and doing everything he could to hide it. As I read Mel's story, I had flashbacks to my conversations with Ron and felt Mel described what my own brother must have experienced as a teenager. Living with fear and guilt consumed their lives and overwhelmed both of them. Mel describes his desire to serve God as a teenager. He was extremely gifted and rose to leadership positions within his church youth group and his high school, all the while trying to suppress and hide his fears. He could never talk to anyone about what he was experiencing and just hoped this would all pass. He prayed and made promises to God that he felt he could not keep. Eventually he took on more public leadership roles in college and professionally. He married, had children, later divorced, and made the decision to go public with his story and could now be described as a gay activist. Even though I disagree with Mel's decisions and conclusions, I found his poignant story helpful for increasing my own understanding of another person's troubled journey.

For me, the root causes surrounding homosexuality or, "disordered desire," falls into the realm of mystery. There are, no doubt, numerous reasons for its manifestation. Many Christians seem to lack understanding and knowledge about the devastating effects of what theologians call, "living in a fallen world." It is difficult for many of us to grasp the impact of the Fall and how it touches every one of us. All of creation bears the mark of the Fall (Gen 3, Rom 5:12–21). From sickness, disease, violence, war, and our scarred environment, we see its evidence. As a result of our rebellious attitudes, we practice a form of idolatry—self-rule instead of God's rule—and let our passions reign. Sin permeates our world and affects all of us. The good news of the gospel is that Jesus loved us in spite of our rebellion and sin and came to this earth to bring us hope and freedom from bondage to our obsessions and misguided passions.

Dr. Richard B. Hays, professor of New Testament at Duke University Divinity School, reflects a cogent and intelligent understanding of this rebellion against God in his chapter on homosexuality in *The Moral Vision of the New Testament*. He writes, "Rebellion against this Creator who may be understood and seen in the things that he has made is made palpable in the flouting of sexual distinctions that are fundamental to God's creative design." (Gen 1–3)[1]

I believe homosexual activity is forbidden in Scripture and is not what God intends for men and women. My heart aches for those who feel trapped and tell us they never chose their orientation. They discovered their same-sex attraction, and it frightened them. Ron often said to me, "Why would you choose this? This is the way God made me." I disagreed with Ron that God "made" him this way, but neither did I deny his feelings. I cannot explain why someone experiences same sex attraction and others do not. The central question for me is what one does with these inclinations in response to biblical teaching that forbids homosexual practice (Lev 18:22; 20:13; Rom 1:21–27; I Cor 6:9–11; I Tim 1:8–11). Scripture also forbids adultery, drunkenness, lust, greed, gluttony, and covetousness. Some of my Christian brothers and sisters often appear to be focusing on homosexuality to the exclusion of these other sins that we sometimes fall prey to. We are not left without guidance. Provision for how to live our lives amid these struggles and issues is provided for us throughout Scripture.

1. Hays, *Moral Vision of the New Testament*, 386.

I believe many in the LGBT community are not aware their "flouting of sexual distinctions" is a form of rebellion against God's moral law. One way God uses to help them understand this truth comes through the Holy Spirit empowering Christians who have personal friendships within the LGBT community to lovingly express and live out God's Word before them.

We need to carefully evaluate our tendency to say, "Just choose not to be gay." Most in the gay community would respond, "I never chose to be gay. This is who I am." Two different views predominate among Christians (perhaps even more). The first view held by some Christian men and women teaches that being LGBT is a sexual orientation that cannot be changed. They would argue their understanding of Scripture allows them to be involved in a *monogamous* gay relationship because this is their "natural" inclination or orientation. The second view held by LGBT Christians affirms celibacy because they believe God's Word forbids homosexual acts and their heart's desire is to be dedicated to Jesus and obedient to his Word. Some who remain celibate find that over time they discover they have a heterosexual attraction, while others find that not to be a part of their experience. Wesley Hill, author of *Washed and Waiting: Homosexuality and Faithfulness*, is one who identifies as a gay Christian who lives a celibate life. He vividly captures his personal struggle when he writes:

> My homosexuality, my exclusive attraction to other men, my grief over it and my repentance, my halting effort to live fittingly in the grace of Christ and the power of the spirit—gradually I am learning not to view all of these things as confirmations of my rank corruption and hypocrisy. I am instead, slowly but surely, learning to view that journey—of struggle, failure, repentance, restoration, renewal in joy, and persevering, agonized obedience—as what it looks like for the Holy Spirit to be transforming me on the basis of Christ's cross and his Easter morning triumph over death.[2]

2 Hill, *Washed and Waiting*, 145.

There are Christians, like Wesley Hill, who find they face this same reality in their personal lives on a daily basis. What should they do? They are celibate, and based on their understanding of what Scripture teaches they choose to practice self-control in this expression of their sexuality and submit themselves to the Lordship of Jesus Christ. They are deeply committed Christians who are compassionate, gifted, and used by God. They continually pray to God for wisdom and direction. With a support network of family members, friends, and a committed church community, they are living lives of faithfulness, holiness and obedience. Is it easy? By no means. They struggle, and yes, they occasionally slip, just as other Christians, like me, slip in various areas, but they move forward and experience powerful lives filled with purpose, ministry, and fellowship with God. They now seek to glorify God in their bodies, because they realize they belong to a Savior who deeply loves them and they no longer belong to themselves.

When Ron was in high school, active in the church youth group, and awakening to his sexuality, he was frightened. But, who could he talk to? Homosexuality wasn't openly talked about in most evangelical churches in the sixties so where could he go with his questions and fears? Where could he feel safe? One of my concerns is that pastors, youth pastors, parents, church leaders, and other counselors have the courage to find appropriate ways to talk about these issues in non-threatening situations that help young men and women distinguish between levels of sexual curiosity, including same-sex attraction, instead of immediately self-identifying as gay or lesbian. Young people need to understand the difference between temptation and then acting on that temptation with the latter being sin. Being proactive and addressing these issues may generate criticism in some circles but it is necessary for leaders to take a stand for the sake of young people who are confused and frightened. Some individuals need reassurance that just because they experience a fleeting attraction to the same sex, does not mean they are gay, but their feelings are temporary and will soon pass. For some, this is true. For others it may not pass. One has to be careful about labeling an individual as LGBT during pubescence or adolescence. One Christian counselor told me she never labels anyone LGBT just because they admit to a certain degree of curiosity about same sex attraction. Instead she listens and helps her client explore what is happening in his or her life. Our Christian leaders need to be honest with those they are guiding and not jump to conclusions or attach labels to young people. Young people need to hear words of encouragement, such as, "If this is something that concerns you and is ongoing, I am here to help you and support you in your faith walk with God." Committed Christian leaders could help assuage the fears that may have filled a young person's mind. Their openness may help that young person have the courage to seek further counsel and guidance. Through informed and understanding followers of Christ, these individuals could benefit from nonjudgmental counsel. Under the guidance of wise Christians who are honest, present with them, compassionate, and humble, they could safely help them face their doubts and concerns. Their shame, fear, and anxiety could be addressed in a loving environment supported by those who do not see them as strange or despised by God, but rather young people made in the image of God, living in a fallen world, and dearly loved by the Savior.

Living in a highly sexualized culture such as ours, young people are especially confronted by celebrities, movies and TV shows that glorify behavior that consistently is warned against in Scripture. From advertising clothing styles, cars and even yogurt, sex is the subtle and not so subtle means used to grab attention to sell a product. The pursuit of sex has permeated our culture and we are all affected by it. By God's power and grace we have his promises that comfort and bring us hope. One such promise is in I Cor 10:13. "And God is faithful; he will not let you be tempted beyond what you can bear. But when you are tempted, he will also provide a way out so that you can endure it."

I have often thought about what would have happened if such a person had come alongside Ron during his developmental years. To whom and where could he have expressed what he was feeling? I realize there are no guarantees, but I would like to think that Ron would have been spared much of his confusion, fear, and unhappiness if he had been supported and loved by Christians who walked alongside him, understood him, and with whom he felt safe. Is there someone in your life you can journey with and provide friendship, safety, and hope?

4

CRIES FOR HELP

"PLEASE DON'T HANG UP!" Ron's familiar cry for help in the middle of the night became a part of my night time experience two or three times a week. During the late eighties and through 1995, the regular ringing of the telephone around 2:00 or 3:00 am roused me from a deep sleep. Ron was drunk and the alcohol broke down his normal inhibitions so he felt free to call me, my sisters, and sometimes my parents, all in a desperate attempt to talk and connect with a living, breathing human being. Years later we discovered my elderly aunts in Texas also received occasional late night calls. They never told my parents about this until after Ron's death.

I kept a journal intermittently during those years describing what was happening with Ron and my reaction and prayers for him. Here's a sample of my entries that reveal some of my frustrations and how exhausted I felt at times.

> February 3, 1991 . . . It has been a beautiful sunny, but cold day. The snow is just about gone. Ron has called me three times. I am concerned about him. He has been drinking so he doesn't make a lot of sense and yet he is so sad and wanting to talk to someone. He seems to wallow in self-pity and has such a gloomy outlook. My patience wears thin. He's not his real self when he has been

drinking. He called me on Thursday sobbing because a friend of his from college days died on Monday. I think that is what started the latest binge.

March 3, 1991 . . . Ron called me at 2:44 am this week. I thought he had really lost it. He was so spaced out. I've talked to him since and he doesn't even remember calling. I wonder what will happen to him.

September 30, 1991 . . . Lord, sometimes I don't even know how to pray for Ron. I want to be there for him but it is so exhausting just to listen to him. My emotional energy is sapped and now he wants to discuss this TV program. Lord, you control my brain, help me to use its potential and think clearly and not become dulled by tiredness.

July 26, 1992 . . . Tonight I felt sad talking to Ron. He is grieving and hurting so emotionally. Help me to be an encouragement to him. Lord, it hurts so when I think of his dying. When I hear him breathing deeply I think one of these days he may struggle for air. Give us courage for what lies ahead. May Ron trust you as his Lord and Savior. You know his heart Lord. Forgive me if I have misled him in any way. I only want him to experience joy in knowing you. Forgive him Lord. Heal him. Help our researchers to discover a cure for AIDS. Fill me with your Spirit as I talk to him.

Writing out my prayers and anguish in a journal helped me to release some of the stress I was feeling as I walked through new territory during those emotionally charged years. Reading my journal entries during that turbulent period is a bit uncomfortable and yet I am grateful I managed to record my struggles and what was happening in my relationship with Ron.

Some of the topics and life events we discussed over the phone allowed Ron to share with me what was important to him. One time he told me about a vacation to Barbados he took with his partner. While there he met an older woman from England who became his friend. During our phone conversations he often described the calls he had placed to her, usually when he was sober but sometimes drunk, and often in the middle of the night. He proudly told me about their friendship and how she had knitted a colorful sweater for him and " . . . shipped it all the way from England." I thought it was kind of this woman to respond to Ron in this way. It was such an emotionally painful time for him, and for those of us who loved him and knew about his HIV status. We were thankful for any experience that seemed to lift his spirits.

In the early years of AIDS many of the anti-retroviral meds used today were not available. AZT (Azidothymidine) was the first drug approved for treatment of HIV and delays the progression of the disease. In combination with other drugs it has a tremendous effect. I believe this is one of the reasons Ron survived 11 years of living with HIV after his diagnosis. Ron received insurance coverage through his work and eventually qualified for disability. He was extremely thankful for good coverage as his dosage of AZT was approximately $2,000 a month.

Ron's calls became even more intense following his diagnosis and he began to drink heavily. It was during this time he told my parents that he was gay and HIV positive. My mother later told me that my dad and she had wondered over the years if Ron could be gay, but they were never able to voice their suspicion to my sisters or to me. She said she was sad and disappointed when Ron told her because this meant he would never have a wife or children. She told me my dad blamed himself for Ron's "problems," but he never discussed Ron's being gay with me or my siblings, or anyone else as far as we knew. In spite of their many differences over the years, my dad was there for Ron and I am grateful he gave him the gift of his presence and financial assistance when needed. One of the most important steps parents or loved ones can take to significantly help their LGBT son or daughter is never to abandon them. In Matthew 25:35–40 Jesus instructs his disciples about the type of acts for which they will be judged.

> For I was hungry and you gave me something to eat, I
> was thirsty and you gave me something to drink, I was a
> stranger and you invited me in, I needed clothes and you
> clothed me, I was sick and you looked after me, I was in

prison and you came to visit me. Then the righteous will answer him, 'Lord when did we see you hungry and feed you, or thirsty and give you something to drink? When did we see you a stranger and invite you in, or needing clothes and clothe you? When did we see you sick or in prison and go to visit you?' . . . I tell you the truth, whatever you did for one of the least of these brothers of mine, you did for me.

We can be the hands and feet of Jesus to our loved one.

During the years of being HIV positive, Ron continued to work as a produce manager for a local independent grocer, but on occasion his alcoholism was so severe he could not function. Eventually he had to admit to his supervisor his problem with alcohol. To the store's credit, they valued Ron's work and wanted to help him. Ron had been one of their faithful employees and they moved him to another position that was less stressful to help him cope during those days.

On March 19, 1993 I wrote a prayer in my journal. I continued to pour out my concerns about Ron.

> Father, Ron called again. He's so scared and lonely and is drinking again. Help him through this. May he listen to others. He's not very pleasant to talk to when he's like this, which is more and more often. May his eyes be opened to the truth. As I think back, it seems his life has been one of turmoil and fear since he was a child. Lord, forgive me for any actions toward Ron that hurt him emotionally. Oh, that he could experience your peace.

I longed for him to find strength and peace in a relationship with God.

As Ron's illness progressed, he began dealing with a variety of health issues that were uncomfortable and sometimes frightening. His CD4 T-cell count dropped. A lowered count is an indication of a worsening prognosis. The normal T-cell range varies between 500 to 1,000. At the time Ron was diagnosed HIV positive, the Center for Disease Control had changed their definition of AIDS to anyone who had a CD4 count of 200 or below. Ron's count was slightly over 200. At the time of Ron's last infection his T-cell helper count was down to 4. The online article, "Understanding the Basic Facts About HIV/AIDS," provides a good overview of the virus, its causes, how it is transmitted, and what happens to the body's immune system.[1]

1. Robinson. "Understanding HIV/AIDS."n.p. [cited 2015]. Although the terms HIV and AIDS are used frequently in the media, there may be those who do not understand the virus and its origins. AIDS (acquired immune deficiency syndrome) isn't a disease in itself; rather, AIDS is a condition that develops when a person's body has been weakened by HIV (the human immunodeficiency virus). HIV is found in blood and sexual fluids and spreads mainly through unprotected sexual contact and the sharing of hypodermic needles and equipment.

When a person becomes infected with HIV, it damages his or her immune system, leading to immunodeficiency; the immune system can no longer fight off common germs and pathogens, so a person infected with HIV becomes ill from diseases that don't usually affect someone without HIV.

It can take HIV many years to damage the immune system enough to make the person vulnerable to these diseases, called opportunistic infection. These infections, including Kaposi's sarcoma, a form of skin cancer, take the opportunity to invade because they don't' encounter resistance. When doctors see someone with one of these diseases, they know that HIV is probably responsible, and the person may be diagnosed with AIDS.

As HIV slowly invades a specific immune cell—the CD4 T-cell—HIV uses the immune cell's genetic material to reproduce itself and then kills the CD4 T-cell.

An HIV-infected person may not have any symptoms of disease during this time—called the asymptomatic period. This can last 10 years or more for some people. During this time, the person's CD4 T-cell count is watched closely to guide treatment. The goal is to keep an infected person from advancing to AIDS. Once the CD4 T-cell count goes below 200, a person is diagnosed with AIDS.

The first AIDS case was documented in 1981, and HIV has since spread worldwide. In 2009, almost 2 million people died worldwide, and the epidemic continues to spread. Sub-Saharan Africa has the greatest number of people who are infected. The World Health Organization (WHO) and the United Nations' UNAIDS office estimate that over 33% of adults are infected with HIV in some areas of Africa. Millions of children have been orphaned. The epidemic is also growing rapidly in Eastern Europe and Asia. More than 34 million people worldwide are now living with HIV.

In the United States and the developed world, the use of combination treatments has turned AIDS into a chronic disease. People now live long lives with HIV when they work closely with their health care providers and are

My parents' generosity allowed Ron to buy his first home in Portland. Later he was so worried about not being able to make his mortgage payments that my parents bought the house from him and he made his mortgage payment to them. When he experienced increasing difficulty maintaining stamina for work, he applied for disability and after a thorough analysis of his health was finally granted approval.

Ron began to hibernate at home more and more. He was afraid to go outside. He had enjoyed traveling to the Oregon coast but now that soon became a rarity. His life consisted of maintaining

---

committed to their treatment plans. Unfortunately, AIDS medications are expensive and unavailable to the majority of people in the world living with AIDS. There are growing concerns that some high-risk groups believe they don't have to be worried about HIV anymore. The fact that people now live longer with HIV doesn't change the fact that HIV is a life-threatening illness and can infect anyone who exchanges infected blood or sexual fluids with another person.

What Causes HIV/AIDS? HIV lives in human blood and sexual fluids (semen and vaginal secretions). The infection is spread from person to person when these body fluids are shared, usually during vaginal or anal sexual contact or when sharing injectable drugs. It can also be passed from dirty needles used for tattoos and body piercing. HIV does not live in saliva, tears, urine, or perspiration—so HIV cannot be spread by casual contact with these body fluids. It can be spread through oral sex, although the risk is small.

HIV cannot survive for long outside the human body and dies quickly when the body fluid in which it is contained dries up. It is not spread by animals or insects and is not found on public surfaces. It's actually not as easy to get as other infectious diseases.

A mother can pass HIV to her child during birth when the child is exposed to the mother's infected blood. Breastfeeding does carry a risk for HIV infection, though in some areas of the developing world, breastfeeding is considered safer than feeding a newborn contaminated water.

There are two main types of HIV, called HIV-1 and HIV-2. HIV-2 is most commonly found in West Africa with research now suggesting that pockets of locations around the world are seeing this disease. New CDC recommendations call for combination tests for HIV-1 and HIV-2.

Blood transfusions were once a concern, but all blood products used in the United States today are tested for several infectious diseases, including HIV. If signs of disease or other problems are found in donated blood, the person who donated the blood is notified to be re-tested by their health care provider and is not permitted to continue donating blood. Any donated blood that tests positive for HIV is disposed of and never makes it into the public blood supply.

his home and a little garden in his backyard. Every purchase was a major decision for him as he closely watched his budget. He rented movies and at night would sit, drink, and make phone calls. He went back and forth between being maudlin and belligerent. On occasion he would swear at me over the phone, scream, belittle my faith in God, and then the next day, when he was sober, call and apologize for his behavior. At first I would try to talk to him during his drunken calls but later, at the recommendation of a psychology professor and friend, I would tell him, "I have to hang up now because you are drunk, but I want to talk to you when you are sober." It was very difficult for me to do this as he would beg me to stay on the phone but over time it did help. I would not shout at him but in a normal tone of voice assure him of my love, yet would not talk to him until he was sober. He began to experience paranoia and dementia that also affected the content and timing of his phone calls. Ron endured some of the same afflictions that other gay men who were HIV experienced. During those years he was treated for leukoplakia, skin rashes, eyesight problems, chronic diarrhea, nausea, thrush, and a fungal infection that led to one hospitalization and intensive antibiotic treatment.

One of the reasons Ron was so frightened had to do with his extreme fear that America would arrest all homosexuals and place them in concentration camps. His paranoia often led him to think his phone was being tapped. In the Portland area in the late eighties a local pastor was leading marches against the gay community with people holding signs stating, "God hates fags." Ron would call and fearfully ask me, "Joyce, you're not like that, are you?" I was hurt by his question, but assured him that even though I believed the practice of homosexuality was not what God intended for his children, he mattered to God, and I did not support those marching and shouting hateful slogans. That was not what Jesus would have done.

One desperate phone call revealed to me how seriously the virus was beginning to affect Ron's brain. He called one Saturday afternoon to tell me he had climbed up into his attic and found a loose radio tube that he positively knew was not there when he moved into the house. He was convinced his home had been bugged. In spite of my assurances otherwise, he kept insisting I write down the number on the radio tube in case anything happened to him. He was so persistent and upset I decided not to argue with him and agreed to write down the number and repeat it back to him. I knew then his paranoia was beginning to consume him and the disease was running its course. Ron was not often this agitated, but when he was, it was very difficult to reason with him. I would tell myself this is the disease speaking. Many of our conversations during that time were quite pleasant and focused on family, life, politics, and faith in God. Ron traveled to Indiana twice during those years to visit us in our home. One Christmas he flew out with my parents and then another year he visited in the spring.

I look back on that spring visit with fond memories. My journal on May 25, 1993, reflects my own state of mind as I prepared for Ron's visit and taking time away from work. "Father, Ron comes tonight. Grant me emotional and physical strength for these next six days. So much is going on at work as we prepare for the next fiscal year."

Ron offered to help me plant a privet hedge at the back of our home during his visit. I didn't want him to tire himself but he insisted on helping. We planted about eight or nine plants with Ron digging the holes while sweat streamed down his face. He paused in the middle of one of our conversations with his foot poised on the shovel and said, "Joyce, whenever I'm here, I feel a peace I miss in other places." I was deeply touched by his comment, and very thankful he could experience a respite from his fears and knew that he was safe with us. I breathed a prayer to God for this dear man to experience God's inner peace and healing. On June 2, 1993, I commented on his visit in my journal. "Our visit with Ron was good. He's a sad man in many ways because his fears and worries control him. When did it all go wrong for him? Father, grant him your peace. May he trust you for everything. Grant him courage for what lies ahead."

As the years rolled by and the privet hedge grew, I often re-called that particular conversation. The largest privet bush was under my kitchen window and one spring a cardinal built her nest between the dense leaves. It brought a smile to my face as I saw the cardinal flit back and forth to take care of her babies. Ron would have enjoyed that too. Whenever these memories flood my mind tears often flow. I pray for inner peace and trust in the God who knows the hearts of all men and women—his image bearers. He knew Ron's heart—his struggles, fears, hopes, and dreams. Because he is a God of grace, mercy and justice I knew I could safely trust our sovereign Lord for Ron's eternal destiny. This truth has contin-ued to sustain me when I have been questioned by well-meaning people who try to understand how I maintained my relationship with Ron. The way I related to Ron continues to be affirming for me as I read books and sermons by Christian pastors and teachers who confirm the path of grace.

I was reminded of this when I read Denis Haack's article, *Trust and Feeling Safe*, in the magazine his ministry publishes called *Critique*. Denis and Margie Haack are co-founders of Ransom Fellow-ship in Savage Minnesota, a ministry to those who want to know more about what it means to be a Christian in the everyday life of the twenty-first century. Haack's words resonate with my soul. I wish I had understood this truth more fully during Ron's lifetime.

> Treating people as those made in God's image, loving them as St Paul defines love in 1 Corinthians 13 means wanting them to be able to trust us even—or especially—when we happen to disagree with them. The fact they may not return the favor is beside the point . . . I need not try to be God, or to try to fix you, or to control the conversation so it ends where I am most comfortable. I am called simply to be gracious moment by moment, because God through Christ has been gracious to me. Being gracious makes sense because grace is the only thing of value I have, and since I received it as a gift, I can offer it in turn, and be grateful for the opportunity, what-ever transpires. Being gracious is possible because in the gospel we have been granted grace, and God's Spirit who

arrives to take up residence within our very being proves
his presence by causing fruit to grow that flows out into
a lifestyle of shalom and loveliness (Galatians 5:22). This
is what inspires confidence and trust, and makes us safe.[2]

At times I felt I did provide Ron with this grace, but I made
many mistakes on my journey with him. God, in his mercy,
granted me additional insights over the years so that now in my
personal conversations with gay men and women, or those who
disagree with me, I more fully realize the significance of Haack's
words. *"I am called simply to be gracious moment by moment, because God through Christ has been gracious to me."* On one occasion my husband and I were taking a short get-a-way vacation to
Lake Michigan. We stayed in a cute little town and saw a restaurant
that intrigued us so we went there for dinner. We had to wait for
a table and suddenly we realized we were only one of two heterosexual couples in the restaurant. We were a little uncertain at first,
but as we were seated at our table our friendly waiter proceeded
to engage us in lively conversation and serve us a delicious meal.
We observed well-dressed gay men and women coming in and out
for dinner. It was a little unusual for us, but I couldn't help but
think about Ron and his gay friends and the fact that each person
there mattered to God and deserved to be treated with dignity and
respect. The evening was a memorable one for us on several levels.

As part of my professional development, I attended a university advancement conference in Indianapolis when I was employed
by Taylor University. At the conference I became acquainted with
Ted who was relatively new to his position at his school and was
eager to learn and share ideas on effective ways to raise funds.
During our conversation he made reference to his partner. He
asked if he could be in email correspondence with me, to which
I agreed. We usually saw each other about twice a year and out of
this contact and a shared meal he occasionally called me to bounce
off an idea or compare notes. When he discovered I was working
on a New York City trip for women he sent me a list of restaurants
and special sights we should visit while we were there. He knew I

2. Haack. *Trust and Feeling Safe*, 1.

was a Christian and respected the values my university held. Over time he sent me news about his successes and some of his work related issues. Ted was an interesting person with a good sense of humor and my first gay friend.

For the most part, I do not know if someone I encounter identifies as LGBT unless they tell me. Regardless, my desire is to treat each person God brings across my path with the dignity they deserve. That includes the lesbian woman who sat next to me on the airplane. This realization has led me into meaningful and fun conversations when I could just be me and enjoy being with the person I was talking to, while allowing the Holy Spirit to guide. My most rewarding conversations have occurred when I have relaxed and focused on the individual and not what I'm going to say. Inevitably, some degree of spiritual content emerges in ways I could not possibly plan or predict.

5

DEATH CAME KNOCKING

RON'S DECLINING HEALTH BECAME more evident in late 1994 and through 1995. Our long distance phone conversations continued throughout this emotionally painful time. I felt the end was near.

A surprise encounter with a tree branch led to Ron's final downward spiral. My parents were visiting Ron in his Portland home in 1994, and my dad wanted to help him remove a backyard tree branch that was hanging over the fence reaching into his neighbor's yard. Dad was 76 years old at the time, and had difficulty confronting the aging process. It was hard for him to accept his diminished energy level and physical limitations that did not apply when he was younger. He experienced hand tremors to such a degree he could barely write or sign his name.

Dad's plan was to climb the tree with a chain saw in hand and cut off the "menacing" branch. Ron was adamant that he should not climb the tree because of his tremors and balance issues. Instead, Ron, suffering from a very low CD4 count and easily fatigued, felt he should be the one to cut off the branch. Having never used a chain saw before, he did not anticipate the kickback and as the branch broke away, he fell out of the tree. He landed on his back but managed, with my parents help, to make his way to the couch in his living room. Before long he knew he had severely injured his back. When I heard the news, I was horrified and, I admit, a little angry. "What were they thinking?" It sounded like something you would see in a cartoon or comedy. Only in the comedy, everyone gets up as if nothing had happened. In their condition, neither one of them should have thought about climbing up a tree!

Following a quick trip to the emergency room, Ron discovered he had a ruptured disc and the doctors recommended he wear a back brace. The irritation this caused to his skin brought on an intense fungal infection due to his low CD4 count. Ron endured several IV treatments with a strong antibiotic regimen that was colloquially referred to as "shake and bake" due to the body's uncontrollable shivering and shaking—a side effect of the antibiotic. This seemed to be a turning point in Ron's decline. By now Ron had been HIV positive for 11 years. Even though he rallied from this infection and was able to live at home alone, the AIDS virus continued to relentlessly attack his bruised and aching body.

In September of 1995, my husband was on sabbatical and I took all my vacation time and accrued overtime for us to spend five weeks doing research and touring in Oxford, England and Israel. By the time we returned in mid-October my parents were essentially living with Ron all the time as he grew weaker and needed their care. Another wave of sadness and grief swept over me as I realized my brother was entering his final days in his battle with AIDS.

The phone call from my mother that November Monday morning was not good news. She described how Ron was experiencing difficulty eating. My parents had been staying with Ron since August. Mom had tried to entice him with some of his favorite meals but he could not digest solid or soft foods. The doctor hospitalized him and then moved him to the nursing home section of the hospital.

I asked, "Is it time for me to come?" My mother replied, "Yes." Early Tuesday morning I was on a plane from Indianapolis to Portland. Dad picked me up at the airport and drove me straight to the hospital. When I walked in to Ron's room, I gasped and just started crying. Ron smiled at me and said, "Don't cry." I was not prepared for what I saw. My brother hardly looked like himself. He reminded me of a holocaust survivor — gaunt, eyes sunk back into his head with lips chapped and peeling from his high fever. I whispered, "Ron I'm here and I love you." I stroked his hand and assured him of God's love. He could barely talk and his eyes had a faraway look. He seemed to drift in and out of awareness. The doctor and nurses assured us Ron was not in pain and they were hydrating him via an IV with glucose because he was unable to eat. I slowly fed him ice chips throughout the day as I tried to comfort him while continuing to reassure him of my love and presence.

During those last days I stayed in Ron's bedroom at night and spent my days at the hospital. My parents had parked their motor home on a side street next to Ron's home and remained there for months. I found Ron's favorite brown, tattered teddy bear he had kept since he was a child and I brought it to the hospital and placed it by his pillow. I also thought it would be helpful to provide hymns for him to listen to on a miniature tape recorder, but he didn't seem to be aware of the music. I asked the nurse to have a chaplain stop by. My continuous desire, or was it my continuous need to try to fix the situation, was ongoing. A chaplain did come by and attempted to talk to Ron but he just stared straight ahead. When the chaplain asked if he could pray for him, Ron did not respond. Questions filled my mind. What was Ron thinking? Was he aware of what was happening? I had many unanswered questions. My sisters, Dorothy and Karon, flew in from California and Montana and arrived on Wednesday at different times. Ron was sleeping when Dorothy arrived so my dad tried to rouse Ron by shaking him slightly and saying, "Ron, Dorothy's here, Dorothy's here." Ron immediately went into a convulsion that frightened all of us as I frantically searched for a nurse. It was difficult for us to see Ron experience this seizure. We were reminded again how desperately ill he was.

The doctor told us the disease had now infected Ron's brain. He had such a low CD4 count that his body lost the ability to fight the infection. One of the most difficult experiences for me was to hear him repeating over and over the word "Why?" The doctor explained that he was perseverating. The infection was causing Ron's brain to be in a circling pattern latching on to this one word and unable to move forward. Questions continued to flood my mind. Inwardly I was thinking about the "Why." Was he asking himself "Why" this was happening? Why am I dying? Why am I gay? What was really going on in his brain?

All that my family could do was be there for him and remind him over and over how much we loved him and assured him of our presence. Since that time, I have come to understand that we provided one of the most important gifts a loved one can give—the gift of presence.

Several of Ron's friends came to see him while he was hospitalized. I was grateful for their visits. Even though Ron could not talk to them, they came. They had experienced the loss of so many of their friends. Tim was Ron's former partner we had met previously, not realizing at the time they were in a relationship. After Ron's diagnosis, he tried to contact his previous partners to tell them about his testing positive for HIV and encourage them to be tested. He later told me Tim refused to be tested. He did not want to know. Tim was a successful advertising executive and I always found him to be warm and friendly but when I saw him this time he had aged terribly and had a gaunt, exhausted look about him. Poor Tim, what must he have been thinking when he saw Ron? "Could this be my future?" I never knew for certain, but I felt Tim was probably HIV positive. Some months after Ron's death I received a postcard from Tim with a photo of himself standing with two women at the Eiffel Tower in Paris, France. He wrote, "Tim does Paris." I silently prayed for Tim that he would experience better health and that he would find true inner peace by knowing how much God loved him. I never heard from him again.

What a bittersweet November experience. Bitter because of Ron's approaching death, but sweet because my family grieved together. It helped me to be with my sisters as we traveled to the hospital each day and back to Ron's home each evening. The doctor told us Ron could die at any moment or he could linger like this for several weeks. All this time I was trying to process the reality that I was watching my brother die and he could no longer speak. It seemed so surreal. Both Dorothy and I held demanding jobs we had already been away from for over a week so the following Monday I flew back to Indiana and Dorothy to California. Karon was able to remain with our parents and with Ron. The day after we left, Tuesday, November 15, 1995, at 4:00 am my parents received a call from the hospital that Ron had died. Again, my heart was breaking as I made reservations to return that day to Portland via Chicago where my daughter Alicia joined me for the flight. We arrived that afternoon and along with the rest of the family immediately began making arrangements for Ron's memorial service, cremation, and scattering his ashes.

The day before the memorial service I found myself staring at a shiny golden box resembling a Christmas gift. It shocked me. I had never seen someone's ashes before or even imagined they could be encased in a plastic bag deep inside a brightly-colored gold box. They were surprisingly heavy. Ashes are small chips of bone. I must have been influenced by some Hollywood movie as I had previously envisioned light-weight gray ashes blowing in the wind. Actually, I never spent any time thinking about this detail before. Perhaps that was the reason for my surprise.

It had been an emotional eighteen years from the moment my brother had confirmed he was gay until the day we picked up his ashes from the funeral home. As we drove back to Ron's home, it felt awkward and strange. My brother was reduced to being carried around in a gold box! I was emotionally distraught inside. I wanted to shout to the drivers in the passing cars, "Do you know what is sitting in our front seat? This is all that remains of my brother. Now he's dead because AIDS killed him." I knew the reality of death, but this was the first time I had personally experienced the death of one I deeply loved who shared my past. I was filled with sadness as my sister Karon and I transported our brother's ashes in Ron's well-used, dark blue Toyota pickup truck with a camper shell attached. Since we had all flown in from out of state to be with Ron, we needed transportation to travel back and forth to the hospital so Ron's pick up became our hospital shuttle and now a hearse.

Those days brought us all closer together. While driving to the hospital each day, we crammed together in the front seat of the pickup equipped with a stick shift we were not used to maneuvering while driving unfamiliar streets under rainy conditions. We took turns driving and reminiscing about how we learned to drive a stick shift. Nervous laughter erupted over our mistakes while we tried to drive the pickup safely and without attracting undue attention. Our emotions ran the gamut from being glad to be with each other to sadness. I almost felt guilty for laughing with my sisters during this time of grief. Like a jostling cock on a pressure cooker releasing steam, our laughter gave us blessed relief. As we shared meals and memories while planning Ron's memorial service, tears and laughter continued to spill over. On one level it felt quite strange and on another, very natural.

Several years before Ron died he'd indicated he wanted to be cremated when "the time" came. He'd wished to have his ashes scattered on Larch Mountain, an extinct 4,000-foot volcano in the Cascade Mountain Range not far from Portland. This favorite location of Ron's has an amazing view from Sherrard's Point. He loved the beautiful panorama of five mountains: Hood, Adams, and Jefferson in Oregon, and Rainier and St. Helens across the Columbia River in Washington. He had enjoyed hiking in this particular area. On one of his hikes, Ron had seen someone scattering ashes, and I think that is why he'd requested the same be done for him.

A few months before Ron died he told me in a phone conversation about reaching out to a Catholic priest he found listed in the phone book. He contacted Father Ed who later became a friend and support to Ron. I was surprised that he did not reach out to a Protestant pastor, which was his background, but instead chose to contact a Catholic priest. I'm so grateful for this priest's care, concern and understanding of Ron's circumstances. He agreed to conduct the memorial service for us. Nieces and nephews began to fly in and we invited Ron's friends and neighbors to stop by the house for a meal following the service. One of his long-time friends asked if he could put up an easel with photographs he had taken of Ron over the years and we agreed. It was a sweet gesture and an opportunity for us to see Ron smiling and looking healthy.

Ron never discussed with us his funeral preferences. This was a discussion that should have occurred months before. During his last days we were all too emotional to start that conversation, and he was not always fully conscious. Ron never mentioned the topic during the months of his decline other than he wanted to be cremated. As a family, we planned his memorial service together realizing there would not be many attending but we believed it was important we honor Ron and his life. The memorial service was not long and included prayer, Scripture read by the priest, and a tribute I had written. This was an opportunity for me to talk about Ron's life, his character, and what I admired about him—his compassion for others, his desire for justice in the world, and his heart for those despised and looked down upon. I wanted those present to know about Ron's love for our parents, his nieces and nephews, and for us, his sisters. I reminisced with those attending about Ron's love of travel, his joy that he could live in Oregon, and his tenderness toward his dog Sasha. By focusing on the things Ron enjoyed and the person he was, I hoped my tribute would help to bring comfort to my parents, sisters, and Ron's friends. This was something I felt I must do. Again, Ron mattered to God. Just as every man, woman and child matters to God. This had to be acknowledged in my opinion. Perhaps psychologically it was also for my own well-being, but I believe Ron's life held significance and I did not want this moment to pass without my sharing his life with others. That is one more reason why I'm writing about my journey with him. Could my story provide a measure of understanding or comfort that would ease the pain other family members experience as they journey with their gay loved one through life and possibly an AIDS related death? This is my prayer.

There were so many memories floating through my mind that week. I couldn't focus on one at a time but instead they were random and scattered. I would lay awake at night rehearsing memories that included previous conversations with Ron. He'd been so excited when he'd bought the Toyota pickup. He'd loved telling me about the camping trips he planned to take to the Oregon coast and all he was going to see and do. There was just enough room for him and Sasha to curl up in the camper shell. Finding it difficult to overcome his fear of being attacked by someone who hated gays, he'd only managed one campout. Ron's paranoia as a result of the AIDS virus impacted the ways in which he could enjoy life. Paranoia breeds unreasonable fears. Stories of gay men and women being hurt physically preyed upon Ron's mind. His fear controlled him to such an extent he became house bound except for trips to the store or to see his doctor. He remained in his home where he felt safe. I think he enjoyed dreaming about camping trips, what he might do when he was well, and where he would travel. Anticipation and hope brings its own rewards.

My parents were always very practical, and even though I knew they were grieving, planning a meal after the memorial service for his friends and our family was important to them. The activity of preparing the meal helped them manage their emotions and energy in a way that permitted them to maintain their dignity in grief.

The day after the memorial service several of us rented cars so everyone could travel together to Larch Mountain to scatter Ron's ashes. I didn't agree with the decision to do this. I wanted to have Ron buried in a cemetery the family could occasionally visit to remember and honor his life. Even when I voiced my objection and the reasons, my dad felt honoring Ron's request was the right thing to do.

Along with my daughter Alicia, nieces, nephews, sisters, and parents, we drove to Larch Mountain on November 18, 1995. Our emotions matched the wet, dreary, foggy day. After parking our cars in the state-provided parking lot, we ventured out to find an appropriate area nearby for scattering ashes. My dad had heart and leg problems that caused him difficulty when climbing uphill, but he wished to be the one scattering Ron's ashes. We settled for a location not far from the parking lot, and Dad struggled to keep his balance on the uneven ground. He nearly fell during the process. My nephew Ed quickly reached out for his Grandpa's arm to steady him. The irony of this moment struck me. My family had just lost our brother, son, and uncle and now Dad almost fell down on the mountain. From my dad's standpoint, he wanted to fulfill his patriarchal role on behalf of his only son. In spite of their quarreling over many issues in the past, they were now joined in this very personal and final gesture of familial affection. I felt I was watching a Shakespearean drama scene unfold before me.

Ron was 44 years old when his short and tragic life ended. Who could have guessed in 1977, the year Ron told me he was gay, what personal agony and pain would fill our lives in the years ahead? Then again, who has the foreknowledge to see the future? No one but God.

I am grateful Ron trusted me enough to share his life and questions during those years of fear, emotional pain, and struggle. I did not have all the answers for him, but I knew the God of all truth who is merciful and just. I grew in my belief that even though I did not totally understand why my brother was gay, I could love him and safely entrust him to the Almighty One, the God of all hope.

In Susan Howatch's novel, *The High Flyer*, she writes a compelling story about a man named Kim who struggled with forces of good and evil in his efforts to be loved and successful no matter the cost. Howatch writes a moving conversation Kim's wife has with an Anglican priest following her husband's tragic death. The priest uses words like grace and redemption. The priest tells Kim's wife, "Was he beyond redemption? Certainly not! No one is, because thanks to the love of God, the grace of our Lord Jesus Christ and the power of the Holy Spirit—the Forces of Light can outplay the Powers of Darkness—we can reactivate our true selves, no matter how maimed and mangled they've become, and achieve healing."[1]

I believe Ron struggled throughout his life trying to reconcile what he had been taught as a child with what he experienced as a gay man. From my observation, that struggle never truly ended. Where did this knowledge leave me? Feeling physically and emotionally drained, I turned to my greatest source of consolation and

1. Howatch, *High Flyer*, 418.

hope—God's Word, the Bible. As Jesus was being crucified with two robbers on either side of him, one called out to him "Jesus, remember me when you come into your kingdom." (Luke 23:42) Forgiveness is available to all, even at the very end of one's life.

The apostle Paul wrote a letter to Timothy, one of his co-workers. His counsel in 1 Tim 1:15–17 reminds me that no one is exempt from God's mercy, no matter what they have done.

> Here is a trustworthy saying that deserves full accep-
> tance: Christ Jesus came into the world to save sinners—
> of whom I am the worst. But for that very reason I was
> shown mercy so that in me, the worst of sinners, Christ
> Jesus might display his immense patience as an example
> for those who would believe in him and receive eternal
> life.

I came to understand that Ron, and others who self-identify as gay, are never beyond God's grace and redemption. The transformed apostle Paul, the one who persecuted the early church in Jerusalem and killed some of Christ's followers, is a reminder to me that no one is beyond God's grace and mercy. In Rom 11:33–36, Paul is overwhelmed by God's wisdom and knowledge and bursts forth in a doxology of praise.

> Oh, the depth of the riches of the wisdom
> and knowledge of God!
> How unsearchable his judgments,
> and his paths beyond tracing out!
> Who has known the mind of the Lord?
> Or who has been his counselor?
> Who has ever given to God,
> that God should repay him?
> For from him and through him and to him are all things.
> To him be the glory forever! Amen.

6

MOM, IS UNCLE RON GAY?

FAMILIES WITH GAY LOVED ones often struggle over the issue of how to explain to their children that a brother, uncle, cousin, or sister is gay. There is no set formula for answering this question. Instead, each family member must consider how much information to provide that is age appropriate and what would be helpful. Be honest when a member of the family asks questions about what they have observed or heard. Not being shocked or avoiding the temptation to speak in hushed whispers will help set the stage for future conversations when other questions need to be answered. Our tone of voice and body language is important as we discuss this topic, and as we are observed by other family members. We usually tend to give more information about the subject than what the child is asking for at that specific moment because we want to make sure we have clearly stated our position. We need to avoid the temptation to provide everything we know about sexuality in one setting and instead carefully determine what is being asked. Addressing the immediate question and being sensitive to what the child or young adult is really asking is the first step. After that, there will be other opportunities to elaborate or provide more information based on what was previously shared.

A question I've encountered is, "How did you tell your children about your brother's homosexuality? Since they were elementary age when Ron told me he was gay, I did not feel it was necessary at that time for me to explain all the nuances of what that meant. Besides, many other members in our family did not know of Ron's status. Our children, Alicia and Nate, loved their Uncle Ron, but after our move to Indiana in 1979 that put us far from Ron in Oregon. They did not have a lot of personal contact with him except for family visits to California, Oregon, and in our home in Indiana. I never planned an elaborate speech or explanation as to how I would explain Ron's sexual orientation to them, but I knew I wanted it to be a very natural occurring conversation.

As Alicia and Nate became teen-agers, Ron's drunken and often frantic phone calls increased, and on occasion they overheard some of our conversations. One afternoon Ron called when we were preparing to leave for an event. Alicia was sixteen years old and getting dressed when she overheard our phone call. As I hung up the phone after this particularly difficult conversation with Ron, Alicia asked me, "Mom, is Uncle Ron gay?" I paused, looked at her and said, "Yes." Her response was, "I thought so." I then asked her what prompted the question. She told me she had overheard our conversation and other comments that had been said off and on over the last few years and put two and two together. At 16 years of age, she knew far more about sexual orientation than I did at her age. She did not act shocked but was rather matter-of-fact. With her new awareness we were able to be more open with sharing our concerns for Ron with each other and praying for him as a family. Her relationship with Ron did not change over the years, and she looked forward to seeing him during family trips and when he would come to Indiana for visits.

Our son Nate was in junior high when he began to wonder why Uncle Ron was not married. He had been asking me from time to time when he was going to get a girlfriend and get married. He recalls me saying, "Well, maybe someday." At that time I did not feel the need to go into specific details about Ron's sexual orientation. During Nate's freshman year in high school Ron's being single came up again. He finally blurted out; "Is he gay?" and I said "Yes." Nate was upset with me when he discovered that Alicia knew before he did—sibling rivalry. Now he chalks that up to teenage immaturity. It didn't bother him to know that Ron was gay. Because of the distance that separated them he really did not think about his uncle often. Later he told me it made him mad when Ron would call when he had been drinking and he saw how it upset me. On occasion Nate would answer the phone and Ron would talk to him, but Nate described the conversations as weird.

As an adult, Nate tells me when he now thinks about Ron and what he went through he realizes how scared and lonely he must have been. "I can't imagine going through most of my adult life knowing I have AIDS. Being told you are going to die from this is a pretty grim outlook." Nate went on to tell me, "I know it was an emotional strain on you. You prayed for him, and you didn't turn your back on him. I hope you don't hold any regrets. It was important that you hung in there for him all those years. I think your compassion for him, was God working through you." Nate's tender and touching comment is a reminder to me to encourage parents and others who wonder what and how much to tell their children, to be as open as you possibly can in your conversations and yet sensitive to the young person's age and personality. The most important thing you can do for your children and other family members is to model love, respect, dignity and compassion for your gay loved one.

When Ron died in 1995, Alicia joined me in Chicago for our flight to Portland. Due to teaching and work commitments, Nate and Larry were unable to travel with us. I appreciated Alicia's support and presence during those days of emotional upheaval and grief. We shared Ron's king-size bed and had long conversations late into the night about the past. I was on the receiving end of the gift of presence and I was grateful for my daughter's hugs, encouraging smile, and listening ear.

In my conversations with others who have gay loved ones, I have discovered that some request their gay loved one be excluded from all family events. They add the threat, "If John and his partner are present, we will not be there." This attitude has torn families apart. Parents are caught between siblings who do not want their brother or sister to be around their children, and their love for their gay son or daughter. The stress of dividing up family get-togethers in order to accommodate sibling requests to exclude gay loved ones can wreak tension and division among families. Wisdom, discernment and love are desperately needed as Christian families work together on how to respond in these situations. What model does Jesus give us? In Matthew 9:10–13 Jesus and his disciples were criticized and condemned by a religious group of Jews known as Pharisees for sharing a meal with tax collectors and sinners. The writers of the four Gospels record numerous occasions when Jesus broke the rules observed by the Pharisees and had contact with people who were looked down upon because they were a Samaritan, a leper, a prostitute or a tax collector. How can we do anything less?

Reflecting back on family times with Ron, I am grateful no one felt the need to issue ultimatums. This was due at first to my parents not knowing Ron was gay. Later, after they knew he was gay and HIV positive, they made no objection to his bringing his partner to their fiftieth wedding anniversary celebration. Chris was always referred to as Ron's friend. As a family, none of us addressed Ron's sexual orientation with my parents except for his drinking and his health issues. My sisters and I talked about it among ourselves because of the troubling phone calls we all received from Ron, but we never sat down together as a family unit to discuss what our response would be. I don't believe my parents ever felt the need for this, and it certainly was not a pattern they had established in our family. It was easier for them not to address it but we all knew Ron was gay and we just continued on as before. I am sure Ron's struggle with alcoholism and being HIV positive influenced that decision. They didn't want to make things worse for him. There was a sense among all of us that Ron was fragile emotionally and physically. I am grateful my parents and my sisters never felt the need or desire to cut Ron off from the family. That was never the question. How could we? We loved him and he was a part of our family even if we disagreed with how he chose to express his sexuality.

Chris, Ron's partner, came to California with him for the 50th anniversary celebration and we welcomed them. Ron felt some of his nephews and other relatives ignored him during the visit and that hurt him. It was like two events taking place simultaneously. On the one hand, we were celebrating my parents' anniversary, and on the other hand this was the first time Ron brought his partner to a family event. My sisters and I felt this celebration was for the whole family and granting Ron's request to bring his partner was a decision my parents should make, not us. Larry and I sat down with Chris during the barbeque and found out he had been a former music director in a church in Ohio and that he enjoyed art and beautiful music. We chose to engage him in conversation and enjoyed getting to know him while Ron seemed to be a little glum throughout the event. Shortly after that, Ron and Chris separated. My sisters loved Ron and never cut themselves off from him or kept their children from him. Even though there were difficult experiences with Ron on occasion, to this day they all speak lovingly of their brother and uncle.

Families need to be honest with each other and to also allow their gay loved ones a voice in decisions. Together, with respect and love, families need to discuss what is acceptable for everyone. In his book, *When Homosexuality Hits Home,* Joe Dallas suggests some specific guidelines for handling these conversations among family members. One of the most difficult areas for discussion for families has to do with involving the partner of their loved one in family activities. This type of conversation needs to occur in an atmosphere of mutual respect where a family member's opinions are allowed to be expressed without judgment. This is not easy for many families but a desire to listen and a commitment to treat each other with dignity and respect will usually lead to some type of resolution if both parties sense they are loved. It could be initiated by the parents, siblings or the gay loved one. Each situation is different, but undergirding all these discussions must be the question, "What is the pattern Jesus modeled for us?" In chapter

8, I write about four encounters Jesus had with men and women who were rejected, despised, and ridiculed by the Jewish people he came to minister to in the land of Israel. Throughout the four Gospels we find a record of these encounters. The Apostle Paul also provides guidelines for how we are to treat those within the church and those outside the church. As families deal with the issue of loved ones who are gay, the pattern of behavior Jesus models provides us with insight and guidance in our relationships, regardless of the issue.

7

The Elephant in the Room

On a beautiful Sunday morning in June 2005, Taylor University's campus pastor was chatting with me during our church's coffee time. I was shocked as he invited me to be the campus chapel speaker in September. My response was, "How scary." He said, "Of course it's scary, but you can do it."

I was free to choose whatever topic I wanted. For ten years I had wondered if I would ever have the courage to speak publically about my brother Ron. How could I relate my journey with him from the time he told me he was gay until his AIDS related death? Deep in my heart I knew this was a story the Taylor students should hear, but I was nervous about revealing so much of my personal life and struggles. As I prayed about this opportunity and sought God's wisdom, it felt like this was the time. Throughout the summer, I began thinking about how I would approach the topic. I reviewed articles I had saved over the years, read through some of my journals, studied God's Word, and prayed. In August I took a weekend and began to put everything together, and it flowed. Of course, I edited and made changes right up until the day before my chapel presentation but the essence of what I had written was completed that weekend.

The first thing I realized was that I needed to cut my material; it was too long. As I nervously rehearsed my presentation, I would come to a certain point and weep. I wondered if I would be able to get through it without breaking down. I did not want to elicit sympathy because of my tears. Instead, I wanted students and the Taylor community to gain a greater understanding about the struggles confronting men and women who felt trapped in a gay orientation, and that family members were also being impacted. How could I convey in a meaningful way Ron's story and his desperate need and right for dignity, love, respect and understanding? How could I help those listening to my message understand that gay loved ones were sons, daughters, brothers and sisters of family friends, the neighbor down the street, or their Sunday School teacher. They belonged to families who loved them deeply and struggled with the knowledge that some of the dreams they had for their loved one would probably never be realized. Two of those dreams included marriage and children—typical parental dreams for their offspring. Some would say those dreams can now be realized with the Supreme Court's decision to legalize gay marriage and the fact that gay men and women can now adopt children or be artificially inseminated and have children of their own. In my mother's dreams for Ron, I knew they included a wife and biological children.

My presentation was on a Monday and I distinctly remember the Friday evening before relaxing on the couch in my family room and reviewing my talk. I was tired at the end of the work week, but as I finished reading my presentation I thought, *Who do you think you are? What you're sharing is too personal. They've probably heard all this before, just in a different setting.* I felt discouraged and wondered if I should chuck my talk and start all over. I called out to God for wisdom and courage, and prayed, "Lord, you know all things. You know the hearts of these students and what they need to hear. I am just your servant. Please use me in such a way that if only one student is helped it's enough." All of a sudden my heart quieted, and I felt a peace settle over me that I knew was an answer to my prayer. I did not hear an audible voice but I sensed that I had been experiencing an oppressive attack of some kind that had caused me to doubt, fear, and question if I had anything worthwhile to share. By God's grace, I felt the Holy Spirit lift my discouragement and replace it with a bold confidence that this was the story God wanted me to tell. That intense experience was a reminder to me that my journey with Ron contained a message of hope that God could use to encourage and help others.

Did all my nervousness disappear as I stood to speak? No. But, many friends were praying for me, and some were in the audience that morning encouraging me with their presence and by their smiles. By God's grace, I maintained my composure. Perhaps apprehensively facing over one thousand pairs of eyes had something to do with that.

At the conclusion of my story, I had planned for a series of images to flash on a large screen behind me depicting men, women, and children from around the world who were in despair, rebellious, and some showing the ravages of HIV/AIDS on their bodies. While these images were being projected, "People Need the Lord," by recording artist Steve Green was playing in the background. My desire was to have the students visually experience the message from this song and link it with my journey, and what could become their journey. The first verse captures the heart cry of Ron and so many others like him, but the verse concludes with three important words that make all the difference—"Only Jesus hears."

> Every day they pass me by,
> I can see it in their eyes;
> Empty people filled with care,
> Headed who knows where.
> On they go through private pain,
> Living fear to fear;
> Laughter hides the silent cries
> Only Jesus hears.
> People need the Lord.[1]

1. *People Need the Lord*. Words and Music by Greg Nelson and Phill McHugh. Copyright 1983 Shepherd's Fold Music (BMI) River Oaks Music Company (BMI) (adm. at CapitolCMGPublishing.com). All rights reserved. Used by permission.

As evidence of God's love and grace, I received numerous notes from students and faculty about various aspects of my talk that spoke to them. One administrator shared how he had a distant relative who is a lesbian and how he always avoided her at family reunions but now he wanted to get to know her. Several students approached me about their gay brothers, their friends in high school who were gay, and co-workers from summer jobs that were gay. The joint sense of affirmation and God's empowerment was both sweet and humbling.

Linda, a Taylor University student sitting in chapel that day, later told me she literally sobbed as I described my early feelings of embarrassment and shock over Ron's lifestyle. Linda's brother is gay, and she rarely shared this information with anyone. She described how her mom and dad and other siblings knew of her brother's gay lifestyle, but they'd never talked about it together or told anyone. Linda was one of the first to talk with me. She used the expression, "It's like there's an elephant in the room." All of her emotions surrounding her brother and her family's situation had been repressed. When she heard me describe my experiences with Ron it was like someone had opened a door and she could finally release the emotion she had been feeling. She loved her brother but did not feel safe sharing this information within her Christian community. This, too, is another grief. When Christian families are hurting emotionally, embarrassed, feeling guilty, or wondering if they have personally done something wrong, some faith communities back away and do not reach out in support and love to these hurting members in the body of Christ. Of course, this is not always the case, and today there are many faith communities who exemplify beautifully what the Apostle Paul meant when he said "Carry each other's burdens." (Gal 6:2) But, if one person, or one family is rejected or shunned because of a gay loved one, we have failed to be the hands and feet of Jesus to them.

In a conversation with a woman from my church, Elaine described for me her gay nephew and the adopted son he brings to their family gatherings. She went on to tell me that her nephew's partner never comes to these events. She does not know if the partner has been asked to stay away or not, but her sister and brother-in-law never talk about their son's sexual orientation to any of the family members. Elaine knew her nephew was gay but never discussed it or referenced the subject with her sister. The adopted son is from an international orphanage that kept the child locked up when he was very young, and now her nephew was providing all the resources he could to help his troubled and difficult son learn to live within our American culture. Without knowing all the circumstances, I could not help but think Elaine's nephew was bringing his son into the family not only to help provide some stability for him, but also to seek support for his troubled child. Would the family have the courage and grace to step forward and act like grandparents to help this young boy while not agreeing with their son's lifestyle or the decision he had made to adopt?

Maureen was another college student who met with me to talk about her younger brother who was gay. Maureen deeply loved her brother, and so did her Christian mom and dad. John was a very bright teenager who was open to his family about his homosexuality. Maureen's parents were filled with questions and emotional pain. They'd joined a support group for parents with a gay or lesbian son or daughter. They loved their teen-age son and yet believed the practice of homosexuality was wrong. I had the privilege of meeting Maureen's parents, and I saw the pain in their eyes. They struggled over how to set up rules and guidelines they felt they needed to establish regarding behavior and boundaries they considered appropriate in their home. Together they agreed on how they would continue to provide a safe and loving environment for their son while asking him to respect their convictions.

With Maureen's initiative, we formed a support group at Taylor University for students who had family members or friends who were gay. It was a small group, but we usually met once a month at 10:00 pm in a private area away from the residence halls. Our goal was to create a safe environment where we could talk about anything that mattered to us. One of Taylor University's professors came and told us about her experiences with her gay brother. Her story was descriptive of "the elephant in the room" syndrome—everyone in the family knew, but no one would talk about it.

Sam, another young man in the group, described his dad "coming out" to the family and the subsequent "friendly" divorce. He loved his dad and tried to maintain a relationship with him. Sam's dad felt he had not been fair to his wife and that she should be free to move on with her life—hence the divorce and a major adjustment for everyone in his family.

As a result of going public with my story, some students were helped to go public with theirs. A prospective Taylor student and her mother listened to my chapel message over Taylor's website and wanted to meet me when they visited campus for their Admissions interview. I was pleasantly surprised when they showed up in my office. They were very open with me about the divorce that had occurred when the student's dad "came out" about his homosexuality. I asked this young woman how she felt about this information. She responded that it was difficult, but she knew her dad loved her. It was most embarrassing to her, however, when he showed up at some school events with his partner.

Throughout the years I have heard numerous stories that caused me to weep and sometimes laugh. Each family with a gay loved one has its own unique story. I have often heard people express their dismay when they discover this information because they do not know what to say to the family member. The most important help we bring to these situations is the gift of listening and presence. Do not run away, literally or emotionally. Far more appreciated than clichés are hugs and a gentle touch when appropriate. Follow that up with heartfelt words of love expressed in some meaningful way.

Lauren was a beautiful, young Taylor student who worked for me as a Student Ambassador. Student Ambassadors helped with calling alumni and friends on behalf of Taylor University and represented the school at selected alumni events and campus dinners. I had asked the student calling team to pray for Ron in 1994 and 1995, as his health had become more and more precarious. I was beginning to feel more comfortable talking about Ron's sexual orientation, and I shared my concerns with friends and some of my colleagues.

I was startled one day when Lauren came to me and told me her brother was also gay. I will never forget her question. "If I'm nice to him, will he think I approve of his being gay?" Lauren expressed her fear and uncertainty with how she should relate to her gay brother. Like many other Christians, she struggled with mixed messages she received from her church and what she had heard from well-known Christian leaders. She told me she felt guilty after meeting her brother and his partner for dinner and realizing she liked him. My response was to point her to the pattern Jesus models for us in the New Testament. We see this in his interaction with the Samaritan woman at the well who had been married to five husbands (John 4); the woman taken in adultery (John 7:53–8:11); the sinful woman who anointed Jesus' feet with perfume (Luke 7:36–50); the despised tax collector Zacchaeus (Luke 19:1–10); and rejected lepers who sought healing. Jesus did not shout at them, berate them, turn them away or ignore their cries for help, but instead welcomed them with a message of hope and love that transformed their lives. I will explore several of these encounters in more depth in chapter 8.

Mixed messages from some fringe Christian leaders have confused and frightened their constituents. Their activities sometimes include special marches, carrying signs, and calling names, all of which only heightens the perceived hostility that exists between members of the gay community and evangelical Christians. This practice shuts the door to opportunities to communicate in a meaningful way the love of Christ. A Christian counselor once shared with me that she encourages people to be very careful verbalizing the phrase *love the sinner, hate the sin* to their friend or loved one. When you're dealing with an evangelical Christian audience your meaning is usually understood, but non-Christians and those who identify as being gay do not easily separate behavior and sexual orientation from who they perceive themselves to be. For many, saying that you "hate the sin" basically means you "hate" them. Loving the person and hating the sin is often what family and friends have difficulty communicating in appropriate ways. To tell a gay friend or relative that is what you are trying to do usually isn't helpful.

Scot McKnight, author of *Embracing Grace: A Gospel for All of Us,* writes:

> It is true that humans are sinners, and we can surely act out the worst imaginable sins. But focusing on human sinfulness goes contrary to the grain of the Bible, which clearly sees humans as Eikons (made in the image of God) in need of restoration to be sure, but the object of God's special love.[2]

Fear drives some Christians to act in an insulting manner because they don't want anyone to doubt they totally disapprove of this behavior. When we do this, we are really saying, "I don't believe the Holy Spirit can convict and intervene in this person's life." If we look at the life of Jesus, his relationship with Zacchaeus certainly did not meet with the approval of the Pharisees (Luke 19). Jesus took the risk of disapproval by religious leaders because he cared deeply for the soul of this man. Love compelled him to share the Good News over and over again with those who were despised, looked down upon, and yes, who were sinners. Does the love of Jesus compel us to come alongside the gay son, daughter, brother, sister, friend, or neighbor?

While reading and hearing about the stories of gays and lesbians whose lives were transformed, I saw a similar theme running through each story. Each person had been impacted by love, mercy, and grace extended by a follower of Jesus. In every instance, these men and women met Christians who treated them with dignity and respect, enjoyed their company, invited them to family events, and shared their lives with them. Discussions would often follow that led them to talk about Christ's love and what it meant to know the Savior. These men and women felt safe because they had experienced genuine friendship, and the Holy Spirit brought conviction and true repentance.

2 McKnight, *Embracing Grace,* 126.

8

EXTENDING GRACE AND MERCY

GOD REVEALS HIS GRACE in the most unlikely places. Just when I think a situation or individual is beyond redemption, I encounter a story or person who totally shreds my idea about how God can or should work in a person's life. Without our realizing it, God is working in the lives of men and women in unusual and sometimes very ordinary ways. I love that about God. I can't put him in a box and make him fit my prescribed method for how he should work in the hearts of human beings.

Rosaria Champagne Butterfield is only one example of how God's grace, manifested through Christians who really understand what it means to reflect the love of Jesus, can be transformed. I first came across Rosaria's story and testimony in *Christianity Today's* magazine.[1] Later I had to purchase her book to discover in more detail all that had transpired in her life. Her book is titled *The Secret Thoughts of an Unlikely Convert.* What intrigued me early on was the title to her testimony—*My Train Wreck Conversion* along with a clip that read, "As a leftist lesbian professor, I despised Christians. Then somehow I became one." Whoa! I found myself immediately engaged in her story and wanted to read more.

---

1. Butterfield, *Train Wreck*, 112, 111.

God's amazing grace was poured out on Rosaria through a pastor and his wife who were willing to begin a friendship with a very public lesbian university professor who was doing research for her book on the Religious Right. Rosaria had written a controversial article for a local newspaper that caused her to keep two boxes on her desk. One box for hate mail and one box for fan mail. When Pastor Ken Smith's letter arrived she found it didn't fit into either of her neat categories. He encouraged her to explore the kind of questions she admired. She wrote, "Ken didn't argue with my article; rather, he asked me to defend the presuppositions that undergirded it. I didn't know how to respond to it, so I threw it away." Later that night Rosaria writes that she "fished it out of the recycling bin and put it back on my desk." She did this several times. Ken's letter had invited her to call him to discuss the ideas he shared in his letter in response to her article. She writes that it was "the kindest letter of opposition that I had ever received."

At the end of her phone conversation with Ken, he invited Rosaria to his home for dinner to discuss these issues more in depth with his wife and she accepted. That letter began two years of a friendship where grace in action was evidenced in the life of Ken and his wife. Those encounters, and the research she was doing, led to her reading the Bible—over and over again in various translations. She inwardly fought the idea that the Bible was inspired but she describes her response this way, " . . . the Bible got to be bigger inside me than I. It overflowed into my world. I fought against it with all my might . . . Then, one ordinary day, I came to Jesus, openhanded and naked . . . I weakly believed that if Jesus could conquer death, he could make right my world."

This encounter with abundant grace for a woman who was expecting alienation and rejection turned Rosario's life upside down. She is now a pastor's wife and mother who shares her testimony of redemption and transformation through her book and public speaking. I remain deeply touched and encouraged by her account of grace and mercy in action, not just in words. Loving and faithful Christians living out the love of Jesus in their day to day lives revealed God's love for Rosaria in such a powerful way that she became what the apostle Paul describes in II Corinthians 5:17, " . . . a new creation; the old has gone, the new has come."

There were other incredible stories I discovered in my reading. I observed a common thread running through each one. That thread was grace personified in acts and words of love that penetrated hearts previously wounded. In their efforts to protect themselves from shouts of anger, abusive language, and hatred, many in the LGBT community develop a defensive attitude. But then, *grace, mercy, and love made all the difference* in their lives. Caring Christians exhibited the love of Jesus Christ to them. The pages of the New Testament are filled with stories of individuals who were touched and transformed by their encounters with Jesus. Stories like these continue to be written today by men and women who are loved by followers of Jesus who reveal grace and mercy in "shoe leather" each and every day.

The pattern for how best to relate to men and women experiencing deep need is revealed in the life of Jesus in the Gospels. In Mark 1:40–41, Jesus encountered a man with leprosy who begged on his knees that he be healed. The Gospel writer Mark records that Jesus was "filled with compassion" and reached out his hand and touched the man. Jewish leaders declared people with leprosy to be unclean based on Lev 13—14. They also denied them participation in religious or social activities. Some people went so far as to throw rocks at lepers to keep them away from them so they would not become ritually unclean. Remember, these are religious people responding this way. For Jesus to reach out and actually touch the man broke all social rules. Jesus is in the business of breaking down barriers, and he establishes a pattern to imitate for those of us who identify as Christ followers. Just as loneliness and fear filled the lives of many lepers in the New Testament, there are gay men and women living all around us who have been laughed at, ridiculed, bullied, ostracized, and even beaten. Some experience intense loneliness and rejection by family and friends. As believers, we can do no less than imitate Jesus. He did not ask the leper how he had acquired his leprosy before he healed him; he immediately saw the man's desperate need and responded with compassion.

In another incident in John's Gospel, Jesus appeared in the temple in Jerusalem at dawn and sat down in the temple courts to teach the people (John 8:1–11). Some teachers of the law and the Pharisees brought before him a woman caught in the act of adultery. Why did they fail to bring the man also? In their attempt to trap Jesus, they had disregarded the law by arresting the woman without the man. In Lev 20:10 and Deut 22:2, the law required that both parties to adultery be stoned. Instead, they humiliated this woman by forcing her to stand before all the people listening to Jesus and demanded a response to their question about what should be done to her. They reminded Jesus that the Law of Moses commanded she be stoned, and then asked, "Now what do you say?"

John writes that Jesus did not verbally respond to them but bent down and wrote on the ground with his finger. We are not told what he wrote. Some Bible commentators suggest he wrote the Ten Commandments. The religious leaders kept on questioning him, so he straightened up and said to them, "If any one of you is without sin, let him be the first to throw a stone at her."

Again, he stooped down and wrote on the ground. An amazing thing happened. Those who were listening and bringing their accusation to Jesus began to slip away, one by one, beginning with the older ones. Jesus was left alone with the woman. As Jesus straightened up again, a beautiful moment occurred.

Jesus asked, "Woman, where are they? Has no one condemned you?"

She replied, "No one, sir."

Jesus, in his mercy and grace, responded once again with hope and compassion. "Then neither do I condemn you. Go now and leave your life of sin." It's interesting to me that when I hear this verse quoted by an interviewer on radio or TV or read this quote in a publication, the last phrase, "Go now and leave your life of sin," is often left off, and only "Then neither do I condemn you" is quoted. Jesus extends grace and mercy to this woman but he also asks for a response of obedience—"Go and sin no more."

For those who truly desire to make a difference in the lives of their gay loved ones— I believe that includes neighbors, friends, and co-workers—saturating their hearts and minds with how Jesus related to men and women can be transforming. Here was a woman brought before a group of people in a manner not according to the Mosaic Law. She was a pawn in the hands of the religious leaders who wanted to use her sin to trap Jesus into making a statement that would give them leverage to censure him. Jesus would not allow himself to be trapped by their ulterior motive but instead left an example for all who follow him to imitate. How did Jesus treat this woman? Not as one who was to be ridiculed and shunned, but as a human being who mattered to God and deserved dignity and respect. This woman bore the image of God even though flawed by her sin. We all bear God's image, and so do our gay and lesbian loved ones.

Jesus did not condone her sin or merely overlook it. He saw into her heart—her need for forgiveness, her fear, and her loneliness. He sent her on her way but with an admonition. These words became my guide as I dealt with Ron. One of the truths I so wanted him to see was that he mattered to God. He was a man of worth in the eyes of God. When Christians carry signs calling men and women names like 'fag" and use expressions like "burn in hell," I think to myself how miserably they have missed the pattern Jesus left for us to imitate. There is a better way. By not carrying signs or calling people names do we condone same sex relationships? No, but we extend kindness blanketed in grace, mercy, and love—because Jesus did, even when it is not reciprocated.

As I have shared my personal journey of loving a brother who was gay, other Christians have often asked me, "How should I act around my loved one when I disagree with his or her lifestyle?" Basically, I think they fear any kindness or "normality" in their relationship might convey some sense of approval, which may embarrass them in front of their church families or possibly lead to rejection. As my own faith communities learned about my brother, I found them to be very supportive of me, and as a result of what they learned about my life they felt safe in sharing their own struggles. As time passed, Ron continued to tell me he loved me, even though we disagreed with each other over his lifestyle. Some families try to hide their son or daughter's sexual orientation from their church community. Why is that? Are we filled with fear that we will be judged by our faith community? Do we think we must have failed in some way or this would not have happened in our family? I think I felt this way early on in my journey with Ron. Initially, I was hesitant to share this information with our congregation because I was the pastor's wife. Over time, I did begin to share with close friends within our church family but I did not have the courage to ask for prayer about such an intimate subject in a public setting. I'm saddened to say I lost much needed prayer support during those days. By not verbalizing what I was experiencing at the time, my silence spoke to my own embarrassment. On one level I thought I was protecting Ron by not sharing with our congregation. I wondered if those in our church would treat Ron differently when he visited if they knew he was gay. Later, these same emotions prevented me from sharing my concerns with colleagues at Taylor University. By that time the AIDS epidemic was everywhere and I knew my brother was HIV positive. Would that knowledge in some way impact my relationship to those who knew me? Gradually, by God's grace, these concerns no longer bound me, but instead I began to open up more and more to individuals and small groups. I urge our church communities, pastors, and church leaders to stand with families in their fellowship who have a gay loved one and need support and understanding from those people who mean the most to them—their faith community. When we truly understand God's grace, and that we too are the recipients of his mercy, we will want to share our deepest hurts with those brothers and sisters in Christ who will stand with us. When I first new about Ron's sexual orientation I didn't want anyone else to know. It's difficult sometimes for us to understand our own motives and emotions about what has happened in the lives of our loved ones. Are we more concerned about what others will think of us or our family if they knew? Our feelings really stem from pride and we think our loved one has betrayed us in some way so it becomes all about ourselves instead of our family member. In my own case, I think I moved from shock to grief, from embarrassment to shame, and finally to the realization that my brother would always be my brother and his sexual orientation would not change that relationship even if he never changed. Our sovereign God was sufficient and able to handle my reputation, my family's struggles, and my brother's deepest needs. There were times in my journey with Ron when this truth was crystal clear to me and I felt God's provision for all I needed. At other times I succumbed to my own fears and pride, but by God's grace I continued to grow and learned how to be the sister Ron needed in his life. My strength and understanding grew as I began to focus more on Jesus and the model he provided for us in his relationships with others.

In Luke 7:36–50 we read an amazing account of another unnamed woman who encountered Jesus during dinner at the home of a Pharisee named Simon. In verse 37 we are told this woman lived a sinful life in that town and she must have heard through the grapevine that Jesus was eating at Simon's house. We are not told exactly what kind of "sinful" life she led. I wonder if this woman had been in the crowd that followed Jesus earlier in the day listening to him and believing that God loved her and could even forgive her. Perhaps she stood in the back by herself because no one wanted to associate with her. Jesus was a magnet to the people of his day. When the lives of twenty-first century followers of Jesus truly imitate and live out biblical principles of compassion, justice, mercy, grace, and forgiveness before friends and family lives will be changed because they encounter Jesus through his followers and experience his transforming love.

Jesus preached repentance and that the Kingdom of God was open to anyone—not just for the religious or those who followed the rules. I can imagine this woman hearing words of hope and forgiveness in a way she had never heard before. I wonder if their eyes locked as Jesus spoke and he saw into her heart and her desperate need. She knew Jesus was speaking directly to her.

Later, when she heard that Jesus had been invited to dine with Simon a plan began to develop in her mind. How could she show this prophet, this rabbi, that she believed what he had spoken earlier? It was acceptable in first century Palestine for members of the community who were not invited to special dinners to gather round the windows or against the wall in the back of the room to observe and listen to the conversation, somewhat out of the way but still present. One could definitely see the division between those who were considered to be upper class and those who were considered to be lower class. This woman followed her heart and wanted to show Jesus the depth of her gratitude for his message of forgiveness, and she wanted to be a part of the Kingdom of God.

It was typical in Middle Eastern homes in the first century for the host and guests to sit at a low table reclining to the left, stretched out with their feet toward the wall and their head inclined to the table so they could reach the food with their right hand and dip their bread into the common dish or take up a piece of fruit. Into this setting in Simon's home, the "sinful" woman brought a powerful emblem of her appreciation and gratitude—an alabaster jar of perfume—expensive and perhaps part of her dowry. She stood by Jesus' feet weeping with her tears falling on his feet. She immediately began to dry his feet with her hair—no towel, just her hair. It must have been long and flowing. Not only that, but she kissed his feet and poured a fragrant and extravagant perfume on them. The aroma filled the house. Why was she crying? This was an act of contrition and a way to express her deep appreciation to this one who changed her life. Luke writes that the host, Simon the Pharisee, was repelled by this woman and thought to himself, "If this man were a prophet, he would know who is touching him and what kind of woman she is—that she is a sinner." As Jesus discerned what was in Simon's heart, he told him a story about two people who owed money to a certain moneylender. One owed him five hundred denarii (one denarius was the daily wage of a day laborer) and the other fifty. Neither of them had the money to pay the moneylender back, so he forgave the debts of both. Jesus then asks Simon." Now which of them will love him more?" Perhaps with some reluctance and a truculent attitude, Simon responded by telling Jesus, "I suppose the one who had the bigger debt forgiven." Jesus told him, "You have judged correctly." But Jesus didn't stop there. He turns toward the woman and says to Simon:

> Do you see this woman? I came into your house. You did not give me any water for my feet (a huge snub that was meant to sting as this was the custom in every Middle Eastern home), but she wet my feet with her tears and wiped them with her hair. You did not give me a kiss (a common greeting to kiss your guest on both cheeks), but this woman, from the time I entered, has not stopped kissing my feet. You did not put oil on my head (another insult), but she has poured perfume on my feet. Therefore, I tell you, her many sins have been forgiven—as her great love has shown. But whoever has been forgiven little loves little. Then Jesus said to her, 'Your sins are forgiven.' The other guests began to say among themselves, 'Who is this who even forgives sins?' (Believing only God can forgive sins, they did not grasp or understand that Jesus was God in the flesh). Jesus said to the woman, 'Your faith has saved you; go in peace.'

In this story we see grace and mercy overflowing in every direction. What is Jesus modeling for those of us who claim to be followers of his? What does this story teach me in my relationships with gay loved ones and friends? Or, with anyone who wrestles with personal sins and seeks deliverance? In Philip Yancey's book, *What's So Amazing About Grace?* I believe he answers these questions with profound insight when he writes:

> When Jesus loved a guilt-laden person and helped him, he saw in him an erring child of God. He saw in him a human being whom his Father loved and grieved over because he was going wrong. He saw him as God originally designed and meant him to be, and therefore he saw through the surface layer of grime and dirt to the real man underneath. Jesus did not 'identify' the person with his sin, but rather saw in this sin something alien,

something that really did not belong to him, something that merely chained and mastered him and from which he would free him and bring him back to his real self. Jesus was able to love men because he loved them right through the layer of mud.[2]

Jesus saw what was in the heart of the woman who anointed his feet with her tears and perfume, but he also saw into the heart of Simon. She came with a repentant heart and was forgiven. Simon came with an arrogant and *holier than thou attitude*. Our loved ones may not come to us with a repentant heart but they may come with a *searching and lonely* heart wanting to know by your actions and words if you will love them, care for them, and treat them as if their lives matter to you and to God. If we are to be the hands and feet of Jesus to these men and women, what will that look like? Judgmental and superior attitudes fail to reflect the grace and mercy that Jesus models for us. Perhaps this loved one is on a journey toward God and our attitude and response to their needs will propel them toward God's forgiveness, acceptance, and love.

In their fear of rejection, they may put on a façade that shouts *Everything is okay. I'm happy. I'm following who I was meant to be.* In some cases, this may not be a façade. We may never know for sure, but that does not change how we respond. Jesus never forced anyone to believe or accept his message. His grace and mercy extended to all those he encountered whether they believed and followed him or turned away. We can do no less.

Another New Testament story reveals how we can relate to others who live in ways that are hurtful to themselves and in disobedience to what God intends for them. Zacchaeus represented a despised and rejected minority group within Israel. He, too, struggled with distorted desires—great wealth and riches.

The story of Jesus' encounter with the chief tax collector named Zacchaeus is recorded in Luke 19:1–10. Jesus was stopping in Jericho on his way to Jerusalem and because of his reputation a large crowd came to see this great teacher and healer everyone was

2 Yancey, *What's So Amazing About Grace?* 175.

talking about. Like the others in his town, Zacchaeus was curious about Jesus and wanted to see for himself if the rumors were true, but he was a short man and could not see over the crowd, so he decided to climb a tree to get a better glimpse as Jesus walked by. The scene reminds me of what many people often do when they want to have a good view at a parade. They find a high point to get a better glimpse of all the activity. Imagine Zacchaeus' surprise when Jesus stopped at the tree he had climbed, looked up, and called him by name. "Zacchaeus, come down immediately. I must stay at your house today."

The crowd was understandably shocked at Jesus' invitation. Verse 7 tells us that "all the people saw this and began to mutter, he has gone to be the guest of a sinner." They were filled with indignation and dismay. This prophet, this man of God, this healer of disease was actually going to eat with the chief tax collector! How can this be?

Tax collectors were despised by many Jewish people because they collected taxes for the Romans. Darrell L. Bock writes about the Roman taxation system in the *Luke NIV Application Commentary*.[3] The chief tax collector stood at the top of the collection pyramid, taking a cut or commission from those who collected taxes for him. The collection of taxes was put out for bids by the Romans and commissions were built into the collection. The fact that tax collectors are often paired with "sinners" in the New Testament shows how much disdain Jewish society had for them. In Luke 3:12–13 John the Baptist tells them (tax collectors) to collect only what is required.

The Jewish people believed the tax collectors were Jews who had sold out to the Romans who permitted them to collect more than the actual tax due as payment for their service. According to Gary Burge, professor at Wheaton College and author of *Encounters with Jesus*:

> Zacchaeus owned the tax district and had subordinates who worked for him collecting money. We are told that Zacchaeus was wealthy, (Luke 19:2), and we know that

3. Bock, *Luke NIV Application Commentary*, 478–480.

he did not enjoy the respect of the community (19:7). He worked closely with the army that occupied the land, and because he had regular contact with Gentiles through the Roman tax network, he was considered unclean. Tax collectors rarely went near the temple for worship. The rabbis taught it was even acceptable to dislike their families.[4]

Luke records in chapter 19 that after the dinner at Zacchaeus' home, something amazing occurred. "Zacchaeus stood up and said to the Lord, Look, Lord! Here and now I give half of my possessions to the poor, and if I have cheated anybody out of anything, I will pay back four times the amount." Jesus understood the hurt and loneliness Zacchaeus must have felt in his heart, and he was aware of his sin. He knew he had been ostracized by his fellow Jews. Jesus spoke to the deepest need of this man and extended grace and mercy to him. The love of Jesus compelled Zacchaeus to respond in repentance, evidenced by his willingness to make restitution for his sin. He committed to giving half of all his considerable possessions to the poor, but more than that, he would pay back four times the amount to anyone he had cheated. This fourfold pay back fulfilled and went beyond the requirement of Old Testament Law in Exodus 22:1.

The story of Zacchaeus speaks to us on several levels. First, Zacchaeus had lived in disobedience to God because he cheated his fellow Jews. Second, no sin is so vile that it cannot be forgiven. Third, there are consequences for sin that must be dealt with. Zacchaeus suffered personal loss in his social relationships because he had cheated many people. Now he was forgiven, and this forgiveness drove him to make restitution according to Old Testament law.

In a similar experience with Matthew, another tax collector who later became one of Jesus' apostles, Jesus responded to those who criticized him for associating with Matthew and others like him (Matt 9:11) by quoting from Hosea 6:6, a familiar passage in the Old Testament the Pharisees knew well. "For I desire mercy, not sacrifice."

---

4. Burge, *Encounters with Jesus*, 62–66.

Again, Jesus ignored the criticism aimed at him and continued to be faithful to his mission of seeking out those who were lost and adding them to God's Kingdom. As we interact with others and attempt to reach across boundaries that have been superimposed by tradition or our culture, this model is critical. By realizing every man and woman as worth because we are all God's image bearers, we treat our fellow human beings with dignity and respect even when we disagree with their choices.

I am aware there are those within and without the faith community who believe one's sexual orientation cannot be changed. There is an active attempt by some theologians and others to reinterpret biblical passages that address the issue of homosexuality—revisionist theology. Those who hold to this view may accuse me of being unloving, misguided, intolerant, and even condemning. I take seriously the biblical passages addressing homosexuality and believe God can totally transform a life. While believing LGBT *practice* is wrong, I continued to express my love for Ron and reminded him often that Jesus loved him too. I believe Ron's same sex behavior was no worse than other sins that Scripture condemns. Former Catholic priest Brennan Manning struggled with alcoholism for years. In spite of his addiction, he experienced God's grace and was always amazed at God's overwhelming love. He influenced and nurtured thousands through his public speaking and books because he repeatedly shared the truth about his own weaknesses while proclaiming—"God loves you unconditionally, as you are and not as you should be, because nobody is as they should be."[5] Jesus loved Ron just as he loved the men and women he encountered daily in first century Palestine. From the woman who anointed Jesus' feet with her perfume and tears, to the tax collectors, to the woman caught in adultery, each had an encounter with Jesus that changed their lives. I asked myself, *Could I be the hands, feet, and voice of Jesus to Ron?*

As family members wrestle with questions surrounding their son or daughter's gay orientation, they must deal with practical matters of gay marriage, grandchildren who need to be loved and

5. Manning, *All is Grace*, 19–20.

cared for, helping during illnesses or injury, and attending family events, just to name a few. These issues need to be confronted and discussed, not swept under the rug or ignored. Some Christian families have chosen to withdraw and separate from their gay loved one while others earnestly seek to maintain a relationship that is honest, caring and shows respect in spite of their differences. The latter reflects grace and mercy. Decisions about what our relationship with our gay loved one looks like must be guided by the pattern Jesus modeled for us and not based on our embarrassment or level of comfort. As I have written earlier, my husband and I chose to always be available for Ron, to open our home to him, to treat his friends with dignity and respect, and to engage in meaningful conversations whenever we had the opportunity. Due to our living out of state, the only time we met Ron's various partners was on our visits to Oregon and then at our parents 50th anniversary celebration. Ron was a very private person and once told me, "I am not a gay activist." He wanted to live his life without calling attention to himself.

The decisions we made about our response to Ron evolved over a period of time. For the family member who is shocked and hurt when their loved one tells them about their sexual orientation, I would encourage them to allow themselves time to grieve, if that is what they need. Set apart time to read, to pray, to talk with someone within their faith community or their pastor who could come alongside them while they process this new information. I do not want to ignore or slide over the emotional impact this news has on family members. My own response to Ron's telling me he was gay left me reeling emotionally. At first I experienced fitful sleep and sadness, but God brought comfort, insight, hope, and greater understanding over time.

Some families are faced with siblings who do not want their gay brother or sister to come into their homes, or, in some cases, not even be included in family celebrations because they believe they must shield their children from knowing this loved one is gay. They avoid their family member and further the alienation and loneliness that may already exist. I had a chance to have an important conversation with my children about their Uncle Ron being gay that I described in detail in chapter 6. As I responded to their questions, I spoke in a normal tone of voice, no hushed whispers or turning my eyes away from them. This was an important conversation and I wanted them to feel free to come to me or their dad if they had further questions, but I also did not want them to feel ashamed or embarrassed. Since Ron was struggling with alcoholism during this time, and they were aware of our numerous late night phone conversations, that issue seemed to hold their attention more. Wisdom and discernment is always needed in our efforts to be honest with our children while also not burdening them with more information than they need to know at that particular moment. We cannot control or predict every family member's response, but talking together and listening to each other must be a first step.

As I engaged with my brother over the years, I continued to reach out to him as one who was loved by God and by me. While Ron knew I disagreed with his lifestyle, I wanted him to never forget that I loved him, and so did Jesus. Some Christians may ask, "How do I respond to my loved one when it is obvious there is no desire to change, and, in fact, they choose to marry their partner, adopt children, and years pass without any sign that my love for them has brought about any change?" My brother never indicated to me that he wanted to change. Is our love contingent upon our loved one coming to accept what we believe? I am reminded of the Apostle Paul's letter to the church in Corinth where he writes in 1 Cor 13:4–8:

> Love is patient, love is kind. It does not envy, it does not boast, it is not proud. It does not dishonor others. It is not self-seeking, it is not easily angered, it keeps no record of wrongs. Love does not delight in evil but rejoices with the truth. It always protects, always trusts, always hopes, always perseveres. Love never fails.

And I would add, even when the person you love does not respond in the way you hoped for, or even turns away from what you hold dearest, our love must remain constant and we must persevere. We have a record in the Old Testament of Israel turning away from God time after time, committing idol worship, immorality, injustice and acts of violence, and even though God disciplined them as a nation through invading armies, famine and plague, he never turned away from them. As long as there is life, there is hope.

My prayer is that churches and Christian families will provide hope and encouragement by opening their church doors and their hearts to walk alongside men and women (sons, daughters, brothers, sisters) who struggle with being gay or have fully embraced the lifestyle. Who will show them the love of Christ that brings hope and freedom if we all pull away and ignore our loved ones? The Apostle Paul writes in 2 Cor 5:20, "We are therefore Christ's ambassadors, as though God were making his appeal through us."

In one sense, my journey with my brother continues as I read more and more about the LGBT community, about Christian men and women dealing with their sexual orientation, and observing the changes in our nation's policy as it relates to gay marriage. On the one hand I am encouraged by those within the church who are reaching out in love to our gay sisters and brothers who are trying to understand their sexuality and what is happening to them. The topic of sexual orientation is discussed more openly than ever. Our media features gay and transgender celebrities and we see and read about their ongoing physical and emotional struggles while television sitcoms depict gay families in a multitude of situations. With all of this information so readily available and visible today, I sometimes wonder what my conversations with Ron would be like if he were still living.

I rejoice whenever I hear about the progress being made with new anti-retroviral medications and medical procedures that provide hope to millions who are living with HIV. They can now anticipate living a long life if they have access to these meds. The irrational fears that first surrounded AIDS and how it could be passed on have dissipated. There is still much that needs to be done, but I am grateful for the hope that has replaced the fear that dominated the lives of gay men and women in the eighties and nineties.

The voice of the LGBT community is louder than it has ever been and we do not want to ignore or be afraid of that voice. As we have the opportunity to interact with our families and other contacts, let us continue to point men and women to the one who is full of grace and truth who can meet every need they have. Our Sovereign Lord remains on the throne and is never shocked or surprised at what is happening around us. Our world and our family members need to know and to see God's overwhelming love for them revealed in his followers. Paul's encouraging final words in I Corinthians 13 are, "And now these three remain: faith, hope and love. But the greatest of these is love."

As I reflect and continue to process all that occurred during my journey with Ron, I realize I still have so much to learn. In one sense, the journey is ongoing because I continue to meet Christians whose journey on this same road is just beginning. By sharing my experience, I hope their trip will be a little smoother. Some of the roads I traveled with Ron were extremely difficult but, I became more aware of God's faithfulness, his unconditional love, and his great patience with each one of us. I don't regret any of that.

Dr. Charles Ringma, former professor at Regent College in Vancouver, British Columbia, captures the complexity of understanding why our journeys have so many twists and turns in his book *Whispers from the Edge of Eternity*. He writes:

> The Christian journey is far more complex than an evolutionary upward movement. There are strange contours in the road. There are the persistent paradoxes. And there is the mystery of faith. But there is the certainty of the Word of God. And there is the reality of being touched by the transforming grace of God.[6]

Lord, continue to touch me and others you bring into my life with your transforming grace. Amen.

---

6. Ringma, *Whispers*, 11.

Figure 01
1951—Ron is five months old with Dorothy and me. Whittier, California.

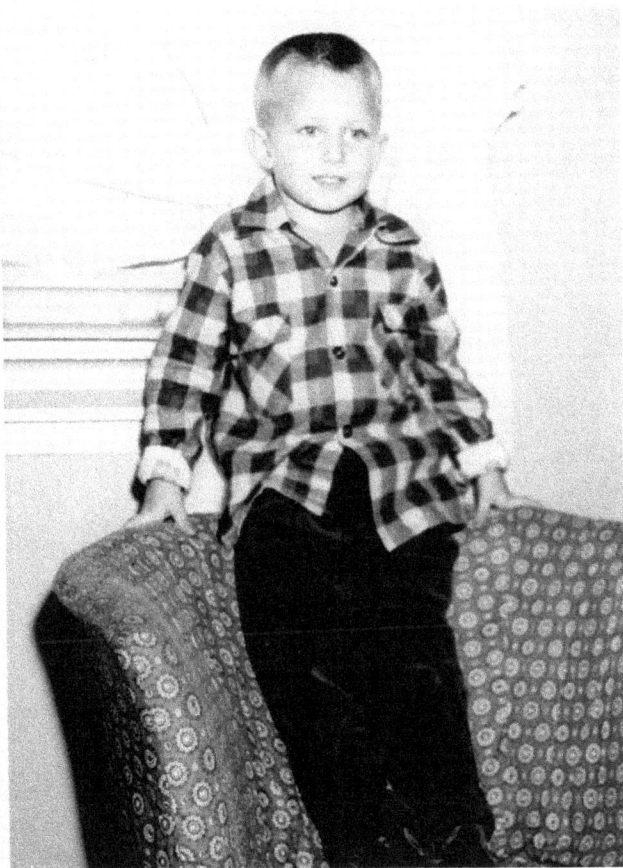

Figure 02
1954—Ron three years old.

Figure 03
1964—Easter Sunday in Brea. Ron (13) with Karon, Joyce, and Dorothy.

Figure 04
1962—Ron (11) with Joyce and parents Doris and Ray Smith family photo for
Brea First Baptist Church Directory.

Figure 05
1970—Ron's high school graduation photo from Brea-Olinda High School,
Brea, California.

Figure 06
1982—Nate, Alicia, Joyce, Ron, and Larry in front of Ron's home in Portland, Oregon.

Figure 07
1987—My mother, Karon, Dorothy, Ron and me visiting in Dorothy's home
in Merced, California.

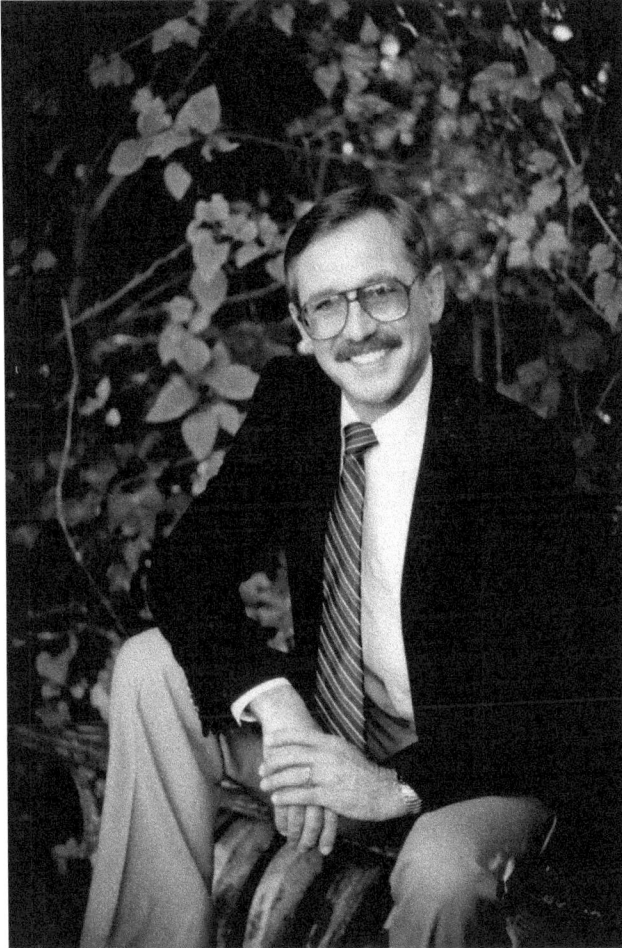

Figure 08
1990—Ron (39) living in Portland, Oregon. HIV positive but not diagnosed
as yet.

Figure 09
1995—Spring in Portland. Ron with our mother at his home. Ron beginning
to show signs of weight loss.

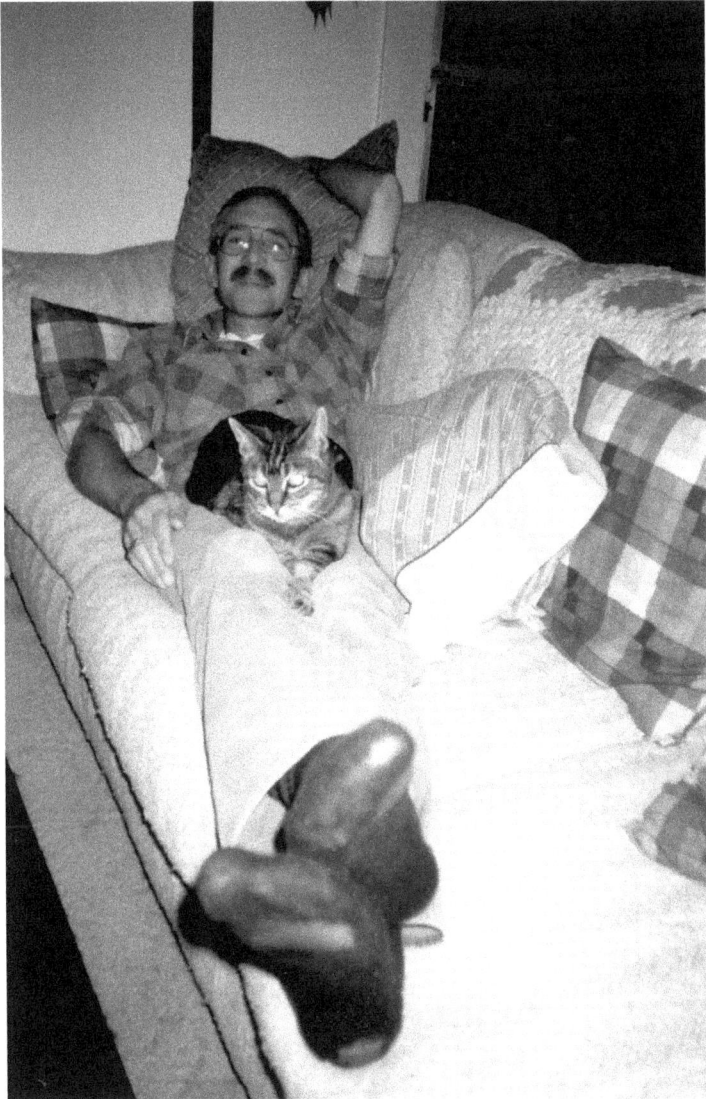

Figure10
1995—Late summer. Ron at home resting with his cat on the couch. He's beginning to experience extreme fatigue and severe weight loss. Our parents spent most of the summer and fall with him as his decline became more evident.

CASE STUDIES

THE FOLLOWING FOUR CASE studies are included for discussion and personal reflection.

Small groups, Sunday school classes, and Bible studies will find these cases useful as they explore together how best to confront situations Christians have faced or will face in the future as they relate to gay and lesbian neighbors, co-workers, and family members. For those who are not involved in one of these groups, the case studies are useful for your own reflection and study.

Case studies #1 and #3 are used with permission from Ransom Fellowship in Savage, Minnesota. They previously appeared as discernment exercises in their publication *Critique*. The reader will find full documentation at the end of each case study. Case Study #2 is based on my personal experience with a family. Case Study #4 is a fictional case study based on a composite of several encounters. All names have been changed.

I strongly encourage groups to process together the questions and experiences represented in these case studies. These exercises help equip Christians confront similar situations that may come their way. We cannot shy away from what makes us uncomfortable or think this will never happen in my neighborhood or to my family. The support, wisdom, and insight gained from discussing this information in a group setting will prepare you for future conversations.

A list of materials for further study provides supplemental information for those who choose to delve into these case studies and would like additional resources. The list is not exhaustive, but it is a start for the reader who wants to explore this topic. Also included is a short list of organizations, ministries, and blogs that offer resources such as videos and other materials.

Loving Lesbian Neighbors

*by Denis Haack**

A CHRISTIAN STUDENT MOVES with his wife and young son into a new apartment. They pray they can be a light for the gospel to their neighbors, and set out to meet and befriend the others living in their building. Among the friendliest is the family living in the apartment next door to them, who welcome them warmly, inviting them to dinner, and happily accepting an invitation in return. The family in question, it turns out, consists of a lesbian couple and their two adopted children. They consider marriage to be a life-long commitment ("divorce is not an option"), believe in monogamy ("sexual promiscuity is wrong"), remember their wedding ceremony with fond seriousness, and are delighted to learn their new Christian neighbor has taken some seminary counseling courses in marriage and family. Though not interested in "traditional Christianity," they are very interested in spirituality. They

---

* This discernment exercise originally appeared in *Critique* #2, 2003. It can also be found online at www.ransomfellowship.org/articledetail.asp? AID=477&B=Denis%20Haack&TID=8. Mardi Keyes's article, *Homosexuality: Speaking the Truth in Love*, can be found at the Ransom Fellowship website at http://www.ransomfellowship.org/articledetail.asp?AID=152&B=Mardi%20 Keyes&TID=7.

ask the Christian couple to pray for them, and say they would love to talk more, especially about how to build a strong family and deepen their relationship. After several more contacts, like the kind that naturally occurs between neighbors living on the same floor in an apartment building, they offer to exchange babysitting.

Now, just what does Christian faithfulness look like in this situation? Since living in a pluralistic culture means that we should expect to face such situations, it would be wise to think the issues through biblically ahead of time. Whatever faithfulness looks like it surely is not merely reacting to the situation when it arises.

Questions for Discussion and Reflection

1. What is your first (knee-jerk) reaction to this situation? Why do you think you reacted this way? What similar situations have you encountered or heard about?

2. If the Christian reports that he doesn't feel free to bring this up to his pastor or to the small group his wife and he are in, how would you respond? Why might many evangelicals not be open to discussing this with sensitivity? To what extent does "thinking Christianly" about these questions require all believers to come to identical conclusions as to what faithfulness looks like?

3. How would you pray for the lesbian couple? Are there things that you would not pray for them? Why?

4. If you would be unwilling to give them advice on building their relationship, why are you unwilling to do so? Write out a continuum as to the sorts of advice that they might ask for, and where, if anywhere, you would draw the line on granting help. (Advice on colors with which to paint their dining room, on establishing a household budget, on setting bedtimes for children, etc.). Why would you draw this line? How helpful is the metaphor of "drawing a line" in this scenario? To what extent are you comfortable with fellow believers drawing very different lines or suggesting a different metaphor?

5. To what extent would you be willing to share with them positive experiences from your own marriage as to how to build a strong relationship? Your failures? Why? Would it make any difference if the non-Christian neighbors were heterosexual? Why or why not? Let's assume the neighbors were heterosexual but confessing materialists (and therefore, according to Colossians 3:5, idolaters). Which sin is greater? How should this influence our thinking and choices? Why? What biblical passages are relevant to sorting out this issue? (Be sure your list involves not merely texts dealing with marriage and homosexuality, but also with Christian interaction with non-Christians in a fallen world.) Also see *Homosexuality: Speaking the Truth in Love* by Mardi Keyes.*

6. Would you consider exchanging baby-sitting with these neighbors? Why or why not?

7. Though becoming Christians would require this couple to refrain from sexual sin (as it does all believers), would it require them to give up their children for adoption? Why or why not?

8. The church is called to be uncompromising on sin, yet to be the most welcoming and safe place for sinners. To what extent have we fulfilled this calling? To what extent is this true of our homes? What might we do to better maintain this biblical balance of truth and love? How did Jesus demonstrate it?

Denis Haack is the author of *The Rest of Success: What the World Didn't Tell You About Having It All* and has written articles for such journals as *Reformation & Revival Journal, Eternity, Covenant, and World.* He holds a Master of Arts in Theological Studies degree from Covenant Seminary in St. Louis and is co-director with his wife Margie of Ransom Fellowship, 5245 132nd Court, Savage, MN 55378, www.ransomfellowship.org or info@ransomfellowship.org.

CASE STUDY #2

Our Son Is Gay

THIS CASE STUDY IS based on a true story. Names and some minor details have been altered to protect the family's privacy.

John and Mary Johnson have two children, Amy and James. This Christian family has been active in their church since John was a little boy. In fact, John grew up in the same church he now attends as an adult and is raising his family in the same house he lived in as a child.

Amy is the oldest child, and James was born two years later. John and Mary were committed to raising their children as Christians. Both children were talented musically and participated in choirs, bands, and various school activities. While Amy was spending her first year at a Christian college, James was a junior in high school. During spring break on a family vacation to Florida, Amy's mother told her James would join them a day later. Amy's mother shared with her that she had found a letter in their home that caused her to question whether James might be gay. She had confronted James with the letter, and he'd admitted yes, he is gay and felt he had been for as long as he could remember. Mary was grieved at this news but not shocked.

Six months prior to this, the Johnson's friends had told them their son was gay, and they'd been very accepting of him. At the time, Amy had thought if that ever happened in their family her dad could never handle it.

James arrived the next day in Florida, and it was difficult for Amy to know how to relate to him. She did not bring up the conversation she'd had with her mom, because she thought it was his place to tell her. He said nothing to her over spring break about his being gay.

When Amy came home from college for the summer, James still did not say anything to her until the end of the summer, when she saw him cuddling with his friend Trent on the couch. She asked James, "Why didn't you tell me?" James responded, "I thought you would say I'm a sinner and going to hell." Amy asked him, "When did you begin to think you were gay?" "This is the way I have always been, and this is who I am. Do you think I would choose this life?"

In response to James "coming out" to them, John and Mary assured James of their love, but practicing a gay lifestyle was not what God intended for his children. James had professed Christ as his Savior as a child, but as he became a teenager he began to question authority, the rules his parents established, and the existence of God and other issues related to faith and practice. He began to pull away from the family during this time.

Trent was James' boyfriend. Trent's parents knew he was gay and turned away from him to such a degree that he spent many holidays with the Johnsons; hanging out after school at their home and was close to the family for over two years. John and Mary set boundaries for James. He could have his friends over to the house, but they could not stay the night. Amy saw James and Trent kiss each other. This was extremely difficult for her. She loved her brother, and her parents wanted James to know they would never turn against him, even though they were opposed to his lifestyle. They reached out to Trent and felt sorry for him because his own parents had turned their backs on him and did not want him around, even though he was a teenager still living in their home. James expressed to his parents how grateful he was that they were not like Trent's parents.

John and Mary joined a Christian support group for parents who had gay children. Mary attended more regularly than John and found much-needed support, even from those she did not agree with. Parents who were totally supportive and accepting of their child's gay lifestyle were members of this group. Mary told her pastor and some close friends in the church about James admitting to being gay. The pastor was not particularly helpful. Both she and John were very selective about who they told.

Amy's relationship with her brother is strong and they are both now college graduates. James identifies himself as an agnostic. He is not a believer, and this grieves Amy and her parents the most. To them the most important issue is James knowing Christ personally. They believe once the Holy Spirit indwells a believer, conviction, transformation, and restoration can occur.

When John and Mary first realized James was gay, they asked themselves, "Did we do something to cause this? Are we responsible in some way?" James told Amy that he feels his family was not open to talking about certain subjects, especially sex. In the years he remained at home after coming out to them, James would disagree with his parents on many issues and test them by saying, "It's because I'm gay that you are saying no."

John and Mary have been very consistent in their message to James, and Amy has greatly appreciated this. She honors them for their loving attitude and thanks God for giving them strength and courage. However, she also knows that her parents' relationship with her brother has been up and down, and James would say they are not close.

Since James graduated from college, he lives in the same town as his parents but has his own apartment. He's no longer in a relationship with Trent but continues to socialize with his gay friends. John invites James to church several times a year, but James tells Amy he wonders why his parents bug him about this, since they know he is not a Christian. James knows his dad loves him, but that doesn't make him want to talk to him about this issue, because he feels he has heard it all before.

Amy continues to have good conversations with her brother about faith. In one conversation, James said, "I just don't understand how Christians can say Jesus is all about love but Jesus doesn't want me to love someone."

James talks about how he would like to be in a monogamous relationship someday and even marry and adopt children. He attended a Christian wedding with his parents, and his mom asked him how it made him feel. James later told Amy that he appreciated his mother thinking about how he would feel in this situation. He said it was weird and they definitely come from a different worldview. He asked his dad if he would come to his gay wedding someday. James told Amy he was shocked that his dad paused, hesitated, and said, "I would have to think about it, but probably." James had assumed they would, of course, be there for his wedding.

Amy wants to encourage people who have gay loved ones to do as much as possible to build an honest and meaningful relationship with that family member, having fun together and talking about normal things that aren't heavy so that trust can be built. She acknowledges it might be easier for a sister to do this than a parent.

One of the things that hurts Amy the most are flippant comments Christians and others make about gays. "It's as if Christians assume that the gay community is completely separate from theirs. They have no idea that people sitting in their midst may struggle with their sexuality. Comments about gay people as a sort of 'outside group' are very isolating."

Questions for Discussion and Reflection

1. What is your first reaction to this situation? Have you experienced a similar situation in your relationship with friends, neighbors, or your extended family? How did you respond to the news?

2. What do you think about Mary reading her son's correspondence without permission? What principle could guide parents as they encounter their children's diaries, e-mails, text messages, or overheard phone conversations?

3. What do you think of John and Mary's reaction to James "coming out?" How would you respond to the same situation? What principles from the New Testament could guide you? Are there encounters Jesus had that could be a model for Christians today?

4. What do you think about the boundaries John and Mary established for James? Are there other boundaries that need to be discussed? What if your son or daughter were living with a gay partner? If they were married? If they had children? Are these boundaries different for a son living with his girlfriend or daughter living with her boyfriend?

5. What do you think James really wants from his father? What do you think about Amy's encouragement to Christian families to build relationships based on integrity that leads to trust?

6. How do you feel about James' response to his dad's hesitancy about attending his gay wedding if he married? Would you attend your gay son or daughter's wedding? Why or why not? What if you were a Christian caterer or photographer who was contacted to service a gay wedding?

7. John and Mary felt their pastor was not helpful to them when they told him about James. What response would you like your pastor to give to those who have gay family members? What principles guide us in determining what a pastor's response should be? How can believers help equip and support their pastor in dealing with these situations?

8. How did you feel when James indicated to his mother he felt he was gay from the time he was a small child? What response would you give to someone who tells you, "This is exactly how I felt?" Is there evidence that homosexuality is genetic? Discuss the current theories regarding the causes of homosexuality.

9. What actions or programs could a local church implement to help its members be prepared to interact in meaningful

ways with gay family members, gays visiting your church or gays sending their children to Sunday school or children's programs?

CASE STUDY #3

Should We Attend This Party?

by Denis Haack⁺*

YOUR SMALL GROUP INCLUDES a woman—let's call her Mary—in
her early 60s who came to Christ a couple of years ago. Her enthu-
siasm for Bible study, sharing Christ, and faithfulness in all of life is
both refreshing and infectious. Unlike the Christians in the group,
however, most of her closest friends are non-Christians, many of
whom she has known for decades. Mary lives in a quiet neighborhood, and a natural extrovert, knows her neighbors well and inter-
acts with them easily and naturally. A very hospitable person, she
has for years hosted annual block yard sales, parties, and often has
neighbors in for dinner. Two doors down from her live a lesbian
couple who have been together for eight years and who take their
relationship seriously. Though it was not a legally binding ceremony, five years ago they exchanged vows "until death do us part," and
have remained faithful to one another. After the ceremony, Mary
hosted a reception for them in her home. The couple is estranged

* This discernment exercise appears on the Ransom Fellowship web site at
www.ransomfellowship.org/articledetail.asp?AID=477&B=Denis%20Haack
&TID=8.

from their extended families, who as Christians do not approve of their relationship.

Now, Mary extends an invitation to the small group, all members of her church, whom she considers her best Christian friends. Her lesbian friends have decided they want children, and so one has been artificially inseminated and is due to give birth in four months. Mary is hosting a baby shower for them, and wants the small group to not only attend, but to help with decorating and the refreshments. Mary sees this as not only an opportunity to introduce her Christian friends to her non-Christian friends, but a chance for the people of God to join her in demonstrating love in a practical way to a couple who are too often maligned and shunned.

Mary was not expecting the stunned silence that followed her invitation, and was taken aback when two members said that not only would they not attend, they thought her wrong to host the baby shower. The discussion—such as it was—went on from there.

Questions for Discussion and Reflection

1. Would you attend the baby shower? Why or why not? Would you help Mary with the planning, decorating, and refreshments? What explanation from the Scriptures would you give to justify your decision?

2. To what extent should you take into account the fact that Mary is a young believer? If this matters to you, why does it?

3. If you would not attend the baby shower because of the couple's sin, what sins can a couple be openly guilty of which would be acceptable to you? List the various types of non-Christian couples for whom you would attend/refuse to attend a baby shower. On what biblical basis is the list based?

4. Most of Mary's friendships are with non-Christians. To what extent are you like her in this? What percentage of your close friendships are with non-Christians? How content are you with your life in this regard? To what extent does it follow Christ's example?

5. How would you try to handle the dispute that broke out in the small group over Mary's invitation? If the evening progressed so that you were pushed into a corner and try as you will, it appeared that someone would have to be offended—Mary or members who were considered long-term, mature believers—which of the two should you offend?

6. Some members of the small group—older, long-time Christians—decided that since Mary refused to cancel the baby shower they could no longer fellowship with her and so would have to leave the group. What would you say to them? Should Christians who disagree over such things be able to remain in the same church? The same small group? Why or why not?

7. Are Christians who attend the baby shower affirming the couple's life style? Why or why not? What difference does it make?

8. To what extent should the possibility of being misunderstood by fellow Christians figure into these decisions?

9. The members of the small group who plan to attend say they cannot believe Christians would hesitate over this invitation. We should be as eager to go to this shower as we would to one given for a Christian couple—who also are sinners. Couples having a baby can use help, this couple, estranged from their families, needs friends, and Christians should be eager to not only attend but to be faithful friends over the long-haul of raising the child. Refusing to extend help and friendship if we dislike their choices or their moral or religious beliefs effectively cuts us off from those who most need the grace of the gospel. No wonder the world doesn't take our claims to truth and faith seriously. How would you respond? Why?

10. We should expect Christians to disagree at times, especially over issues like this requiring discerning choices. What should that disagreement look like, or to put it another way, what does it mean for Christians to disagree Christianly?

11. Some months after the shower Mary reports that she is now considered the lesbian couple's child's "grandmother." To what extent would the evangelical Christian community better reflect God's grace if more Christians were in such relationships?

12. To what extent are Matthew 6:12–15, Matthew 18:23–35, and Luke 7:36–50 relevant to this discussion?

CASE STUDY #4

Sam and Roger

SAM GREW UP IN a committed Christian family and was baptized and professed Christ as his Savior when he was eight years old. During college he finally admitted to himself that he was gay but did not tell his family. He began to practice a gay lifestyle that led him to keep this aspect of his life hidden from his parents and siblings.

Sam became a successful lawyer and felt he had found his soul mate in Roger. He had less and less contact with his family for several years. After Roger and he moved in together, Sam felt he needed to be open to his parents and told them he was gay and was first aware of these feelings as a teenager. His parents were shocked and embarrassed. Sam had a brother and a sister he kept in touch with now and then but they were not close. He asked his parents to explain the situation to his siblings. His parents assured him of their love but could not accept his lifestyle and believed this was not God's will for him. They continued to keep in touch with Sam via phone and email but they were confused as to how they should now relate to Sam and his partner Roger. Sam's siblings were Christians and they were concerned about what kind of influence Sam would be on their young children and chose not to have contact with Sam and Roger.

Over time, Sam's parents began to open up to their pastor and seek counsel for how they could deal with this situation in their lives. They found support, not condemnation and wanted to reach out to Sam in more tangible ways. They loved him and missed him at family gatherings.

During this time, they heard from Sam that he had been offered a job in their state and would now be living closer to his family. He told them he was eager to have them meet Roger and wanted to invite them, plus his siblings, and their families to come to their new home for Thanksgiving dinner after they moved and were settled. Questions in the family began to surface and Sam's parents felt unsettled. They wondered if they would appear to be condoning Sam's gay lifestyle if they went to his home. How should they treat Roger? Sam's brother told his parents he and his family would not join them for Thanksgiving dinner if they chose to go to Sam's home. Sam's sister told his parents that she and her family would be there for the sake of the family and keeping them together.

Questions for Discussion and Reflection

1. Should Sam's parents accept his invitation for Thanksgiving dinner in his home? Why or why not?

2. Do Sam's parents and/or his siblings have the right to set parameters for the evening? Why would that be a concern for them? What could a conversation look like between Sam and his parents that would be honest, yet loving, and reflect trust and respect?

3. If Sam's parents choose to attend the dinner and their son and family do not, what reasons could his parents give for explaining their desire to be in Sam's home? Should Sam's parents offer to mediate between Sam and his brother, and what could they do to help bring about reconciliation?

4. To what extent are we willing to commit to reconciliation between family members who have doctrinal and lifestyle disagreements? What guidelines are useful in helping to launch and direct such a conversation between family members?

5. Why do you think Sam's sister changed her mind and was willing to accept an invitation into Sam's home and bring her family? How should she prepare her family for their visit or is that a legitimate concern? Keep in mind, Sam had a relationship with his siblings and nieces and nephews before they knew he was gay.

6. If you were the pastor of Sam's parents, what scriptural counsel would you give as they seek to honor God, love their gay son, respect their other children's views, and maintain a meaningful relationship with all of them?

For Further Study

Never take credit for not falling into a temptation
that never tempted you in the first place.

—Billy Graham

The following books, articles, websites and ministries are suggested for the reader. Citation of these sources does not imply the author's total agreement.

Arterburn, Jerry and Stephen F. Arterburn. *How Will I Tell My Mother? A True Story of One Man's Battle With Homosexuality and AIDS.* Nashville: Thomas Nelson, 1990.

Baker, Don. *Beyond Rejection.* Portland: Multnomah, 1985.

Bock, Darrell L. *Luke: The NIV Application Commentary.* Grand Rapids: Zondervan, 1996.

Bohlin, Sue. "Helping Teens Understand Homosexuality—Facts to Help Youth Withstand the Current Culture." *Gender Insecurity* (July 2005). www.probe.org/helping-teens-understand-homosexuality.

Bray, Alan. *The Friend.* Chicago: University of Chicago Press, 2006.

Burge, Gary. *Encounters with Jesus.* Grand Rapids: Zondervan, 2010.

Butterfield, Rosaria. *The Secret Thoughts of an Unlikely Convert.* Pittsburgh: Crown and Covenant. 2012.

———. "My Train Wreck Conversion." *Christianity Today.* January/February, (2013). 112–111.

Comiskey, Andrew. *Pursuing Sexual Wholeness: How Jesus Heals the Homosexual.* Lake Mary: Siloam, 1989.

Consiglio, William. *Homosexual No More: Practical Strategies for Christians Overcoming Homosexuality.* Wheaton: Victor Books, 1991.

Dallas, Joe and Nancy Heche. *The Complete Christian Guide to Understanding Homosexuality* Eugene: Harvest House, 2010.

Dallas, Joe. *Desires in Conflict*. Eugene: Harvest House, 1991.

———. *When Homosexuality Hits Home: What to Do When a Loved One Says They're Gay*. Eugene: Harvest House, 2004.

Davies, Bob & Lori Rentzel. *Coming Out of Homosexuality: New Freedom for Men & Women*. Downers Grove: InterVarsity, 1993.

DeYoung, Kevin. *What Does the Bible Really Teach About Homosexuality?* Wheaton: Crossway, 2015.

Foster, David Kyle. *Love Hunger: A Harrowing Journey from Sexual Addiction to True Fulfillment*. Fairfax: Chosen, 2014.

Gagnon, Robert A. *The Bible and Homosexual Practice: Texts and Hermeneutics*. Nashville: Abingdon, 2002.

———. *Homosexuality and the Bible: Two Views*. Minneapolis: Fortress, 2009.

Haack, Denis. "Trust and Feeling Safe." *Critique* 2. (2011) 1.

Hays, Richard B. *The Moral Vision of the New Testament: A Contemporary Introduction to New Testament Ethics*. New York: HarperCollins, 1996.

Hill, Wesley. *Washed and Waiting: Reflections on Christian Faithfulness and Homosexuality*. Grand Rapids: Zondervan, 2010.

Howatch, Susan. *The High Flyer*. New York: Ballentine, 2001. (A novel that weaves a story about Anglican priests helping people who need inner healing and redemption over the powers of darkness.)

Hubbard, Peter. *Love Into Light: The Gospel, The Homosexual and The Church*. Greenville: Ambassador International, 2013.

Kaltenbach, Caleb. *Messy Grace: How a Pastor with Gay Parents Learned to Love Others Without Sacrificing Conviction*. Colorado Springs: WaterBrook, 2015.

Manning, Brennan. *All Is Grace: A Ragamuffin Memoir*. Colorado Springs: David C. Cook, 2011.

Marin, Andrew. *Love Is An Orientation: Elevating the Conversation with the Gay Community*. Downers Grove: InterVarsity, 2009.

McKnight, Scot. *Embracing Grace: A Gospel for All of Us*. Brewster: Paraclete, 2005.

Nouwen, Henri J. M. *The Inner Voice of Love: A Journey Through Anguish to Freedom*. New York: Image, 1999

Ringma, Charles. *Whispers from the Edge of Eternity*. Vancouver: Regent College Publishing, 2005. (Devotional book with special insights for extending grace and mercy.)

Roberts, Christopher Chenault. *Creation and Covenant: The Significance of Sexual Difference in the Moral Theology of Marriage*. Bloomsbury: T&T Clark, 2008.

Robinson, Jennifer. "Understanding HIV/AIDS—The Basic Facts."No pages. Cited 26 February 2015. Online: http://www.webmd.com/his-aids/guide/understanding-aids-hiv-basics.

Schmidt, Thomas E. *Straight & Narrow? Compassion & Clarity in the Homosexuality Debate.* Downers Grove: InterVarsity, 1995.

Selmys, Melinda. *Sexual Authenticity: An Intimate Reflection on Homosexuality and Catholicism.* Huntington: Our Sunday Visitor, 2009.

Stanton, Glenn T. *Loving my (LGBT) Neighbor: Being Friends in Grace & Truth.* Chicago: Moody, 2014.

Via, Dan O. and Robert A. J. Gagnon. *Homosexuality and the Bible: Two Views.* Minneapolis: Fortress, 2003.

White, Mel. *Stranger at the Gate: To Be Gay and Christian in America.* New York City: The Penguin Group, 1995.

Worthen, Anita and Bob Davies. *Someone I Love Is Gay: How Family & Friends Can Respond.* Downers Grove: InterVarsity. 1996.

Yancey, Philip. *What's So Amazing About Grace?* Grand Rapids: Zondervan, 1997.

Yarhouse, Mark A. *Homosexuality and the Christian.* Bloomington: Bethany House, 2010.

Yuan, Christopher and Angela Yuan. *Out of a Far Country.* Colorado Springs: Waterbrook, 2011.

OTHER RESOURCES

Mastering Life Ministries—Nashville, TN (www.MasteringLife.org)

DVD—*Such Were Some of You: For Those With Loved Ones Who Struggle with Homosexuality,* by Mastering Life Ministries and Pure Passion Media.

Probe Ministries—Articles by Sue Bohlin posted on their website are particularly helpful. www.probe.org or info@probe.org,

Seat of Mercy—Post Falls, Idaho. John Forbes, Founder/Director. www.seatofmercy.org.

Living Hope Ministries—Arlington, TX. www.livehope.org.

Ransom Fellowship—Savage, MN. www.ransomfellowship.org.

www.ingramcontent.com/pod-product-compliance
Lightning Source LLC
Chambersburg PA
CBHW060311100426

42812CB00003B/747